Presidential Transitions in Private Colleges

Six Integrated Phases Essential for Success

Anticipating a Departure

Departing with Style

Searching Successfully

Preparing for a New Presidency

Launching a New Presidency

Evaluating Presidential and Board Performance

Robert C. Andringa
and Allen P. Splete

This publication was a joint effort between the following two associations committed to the advancement of private liberal arts education:

Council for Christian Colleges & Universities (CCCU)
321 Eighth St., NE
Washington, DC 20002-6158
Telephone: (202) 546-8713
Fax: (202) 546-8913
E-mail: council@cccu.org
Web: www.cccu.org

Council of Independent Colleges (CIC)
One Dupont Circle, Suite 320
Washington, DC 20036
Telephone: (202) 466-7230
Fax: (20) 466-7238
E-mail: cic@cic.nche.edu
Web: www.cic.edu

Printed in the United States of America.

ISBN: 0-9652730-5-9
Book design by Ellen Cornett, Graphic Design & Production

ORDERING INFORMATION IS AT THE BACK OF THE BOOK

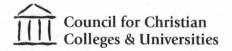 Council for Christian Colleges & Universities

 THE COUNCIL OF INDEPENDENT COLLEGES

Dedicated to our friends who have served in presidencies with distinction.

Robert C. Andringa

Table of Contents

Preparing for a New Presidency

Launching a New Presidency

Evaluating Presidential and Board Performance

Foreword

Presidential transitions are one of the more important events in the life of a college or university, yet too frequently a broad perspective on the transition is eclipsed by the immediate needs of conducting a search. At long last, we may have a signpost to a better way of approaching presidential transitions. Robert Andringa and Allen Splete, in their new book, have provided the important reminder that presidential transitions are part of an institutional cycle. Their discussion of the cyclical nature of presidencies should help outgoing presidents, incoming presidents, candidates for presidencies, trustees who are about to launch a presidential search, board members who are deeply involved in a search, and even those who have just completed a search. Presented in the handy format of many brief, topical chapters, this book is short enough that it can be required reading for everyone involved in one stage or another of a presidential transition. The book can be consulted repeatedly at different stages in the cycle. Complementing some recent thoughtful, scholarly studies of the college presidency, this volume covers essential matters in ways that will orient those for whom the subject is all new, and contribute much to the understanding of the subject by those who are already deeply involved in a transition.

There is not a well-established habit of succession planning in higher education. In contrast, corporations and even family businesses commonly recruit someone into a senior position with the goal of grooming that individual to take over the top job when the CEO retires. Promotion to the CEO's chair is not guaranteed, of course, but it is nonetheless common in corporations to talk openly about expectations. That is rarely the case in colleges and universities, perhaps because in the academy we trust in the ability of a broadly participatory process to render the best choice. It is the patterns of newly appointed presidents' previous positions that are regularly scrutinized for clues about new professional trajectories. The average college presidency lasts about six years, which is to say that approximately 600 colleges change incumbent presidents each year.

Bob and Al bring much experience to their assignment. They have watched over and have sometimes been involved in hundreds of transitions. The Council for Christian Colleges & Universities, which Bob has headed since 1994, currently has 176 members and affiliates in 24 nations; and the Council of Independent Colleges, which Al led from 1986 to 2000, now has 544 members. Many campuses choose to belong to both organizations.

The Council of Independent Colleges is pleased to join with the Council for Christian Colleges & Universities in publishing and distributing this volume of practical advice, based on the experiences of many institutions. It is precisely this sort of practical assistance that CIC tries to offer its members and, by extension, to all small and mid-sized private institutions.

Richard Ekman
President
Council of Independent Colleges
April 2005

Acknowledgements

Two things slowed me down in fulfilling my desire to help small colleges in their presidential transitions: time to write and uncertainty that my observations were accurate enough to put in a book. On the first problem, my board encouraged me to get away for several weeks to focus on the project. My friend Allen Splete came to the rescue on the second challenge when he offered to read my drafts and write a few chapters where his experience was exceptional. As the former chief executive of a sister organization, the Council of Independent Colleges, Al had become a good and admired friend. Thank you Al!

When our collaboration resulted in a completed manuscript, colleagues in sister associations made major contributions. Dan Levin, the veteran director of publications at the Association of Governing Boards agreed to provide needed copy editing. Then Richard Ekman, the current president of the Council of Independent Colleges (CIC), offered his capable staff to move the manuscript through printing into what you have in your hands. That gift of service was led by Laura Wilcox, CIC's vice president for communications. I am deeply indebted to the high quality of help provided by CIC colleagues.

Others who encouraged and assisted me through the research and writing process included two of my board chairmen, Loren Gresham of Southern Nazarene University and Blair Dowden of Huntington College, and numerous presidents who suggested topics and provided insights from their experiences in transition. Early in the conceptualization phase, Susan Whealler Johnston, vice president at the Association of Governing Boards, provided ideas and needed encouragement.

All of my excellent staff colleagues at the Council for Christian Colleges & Universities supported this extracurricular effort. Among those who stepped up with frequent assistance were Lolita Rochon, Maye Saephanh, Carmen Rives, Brandon Rush, and Diana Allen. Other friends whose ideas and encouragement kept me going include Rob Stevenson, Tommy Thomas, Jim Martin, Bud Austin, Merrill Ewert, David Gyertson, Stan Gaede, and many others.

No married writer can succeed without a supportive spouse. Sue never complained when our vacation weeks needed some time for "the book." Her unfailing love keeps me going.

With all this help, I accept full responsibility for the content. I hope that some of the lessons and principles Al and I share here will help boards and presidents improve on the stories of transition.

Robert C. Andringa

Introduction

The average tenure for college presidents is just under seven years. That means, of the 4,200 accredited and degree-granting institutions in the United States, there are some 600 new presidents each year. About half of all presidencies end within five years.

This book is written especially for presidents, presidential candidates, and trustees. Our experience in presidential transitions has come from watching and sometimes being on the edges of hundreds of presidential searches at small private liberal arts colleges. On these campuses, presidential transitions generate more anxiety and require more activity than almost any other institutional change. Some transitions are done well. Most could be significantly improved.

Boards of trustees seldom anticipate the complexities, let alone understand all the key elements for successful transitions. Candidates have seldom, if ever, traveled this road before. Outgoing presidents and their families usually are focused on their next chapter in life. And most search committee chairs do their jobs only once in a lifetime.

In certain respects, the private and public sectors of higher education mirror one another. In a similar handbook written about and for state colleges and universities, John W. Moore and Joanne M. Barrows make these sobering observations:

> *Ample evidence suggests that many presidential transitions are untimely, poorly managed, personally dissatisfying, and in some cases even demeaning for the primary players—the presidents themselves. In some cases, incumbent presidents leave office without the dignity and respect their years of service should merit and without the prospect that life after the presidency can be fulfilling. Often, newly appointed presidents enter into office without the facilitation and orientation necessary to enhance their chances of success and personal satisfaction. Institutions regularly experience unnecessary disruptions and uncertainty about the needs of the campus community during the process of succession and transition. (Moore, 2001)*

This book is dedicated to the proposition that we can do much better than that. Transitions are never easy. Perhaps there are 100 or more "critical steps," any one of which holds the potential to make or break the process.

At the outset of this project, I considered the period of presidential transition in a private institution to be the period from the day an incumbent's departure was announced to perhaps 90 days following the arrival of his or her successor. But the accounts in this volume suggest transitions never end. At any time, certain things done or left undone by presidents and boards can hasten another search. So this book addresses succession and transition as a cycle that needs regular attention.

In researching this book, I studied approximately 50 books, articles, and manuals prepared by people who have served as presidents or who studied presidents' lives and careers. In addition, I solicited suggestions and comments on early drafts from more than 30 current and ten former presidents. I have carefully observed nearly 100 presidential transitions during my four-decade career in higher education. As president of an association of private colleges for more than ten years, I frequently serve as a confidant to search committee chairs, candidates, outgoing presidents, and newly appointed presidents, and I often am an informal adviser to search consultants.

Midway through the drafting, I knew the book would be better if I could entice Allen Splete to collaborate with me. Allen has been a college president and the chief executive of the Council of Independent Colleges, which today counts more than 500 member campuses. He, too, has watched and participated in hundreds of presidential transitions, and his wisdom and experience informed every chapter.

Our focus on this topic leaves us with the hope that others will take up the challenge to research this area so critical to the future of private higher education. We need more professional associations offering help to prospective presidents, to newly appointed presidents and their spouses, and to those who have decided it is time to leave the presidency. Board chairs and search committee chairs also need help when the hour comes for critical decisions. There are many legal, financial, operational, and emotional dimensions to presidential transitions that beg for greater attention.

One key to benefiting from this book is to remember that no two transitions are the same. In fact, every close observer is amazed at how uniquely every transition unfolds. So we have looked for principles that seem to be important in most transitions while offering some ideas that may stimulate creative approaches.

Our great hope is that this book will provide a roadmap for those who find themselves driving the process of presidential transition. Each section attempts to capture the main elements of one part of the transition life-cycle, a process we suggest never ends. There is no "first" section. Wherever you may be in this cycle is where we urge you to begin reading.

Robert C. Andringa, Ph.D.
Washington, D.C.
April 2005

Anticipating a Departure

Chapter 1
Why Presidents Leave

If we really understood why presidents leave, some presidencies could be saved. Others could have their successes enhanced and their tenures extended a few years. And some unsuccessful presidencies might be terminated earlier with more grace and honor if we knew more of the cyclical dynamics of succession and transition.

According to the American Council on Education, half of all presidencies last six years or less. A longitudinal study by Bruce Alton and Kathleen Lis Dean of the reasons presidents leave provides insights for presidents and boards alike (Alton, Dean 2002). Although their study was not limited to private college presidents, Alton and Dean could not identify any significant differences between the two sectors.

Providing context for this book, Alton and Dean's study broke down the reasons presidents leave.

- 40 percent retire

- 32 percent resign to take another position, but not a presidency

- 25 percent resign to accept another college or university presidency

- 3 percent die in office

Except for those who die unexpectedly, both the board and the presidents influence the when, why, and how of each departure. We will look at all angles of these transitions.

Alton and Dean's research provided valuable insights into the reasons one-third of the departing presidents left at an average age of 57 after an average 8.4 years in office (exceeding the median 6.9 years for the typical departure) for jobs other than another presidency. With the exception of number 9 in the list of reasons below, there should be few differences between public and private college presidents in this 2001 survey. Here are reasons presidents gave for leaving their presidencies:

1. Accepted a better job

2. Accomplished all the major goals I set out to achieve

3. (Tied for second) Was unable to lead because of intractable forces such as frustration with the board, litigation, turf fights with the faculty

4. Physical and emotional exhaustion

5. Tired of working with resistant faculty

6. The board was divided, micromanaged, not involved in fund-raising

7. Always thought ten years was the maximum I wanted to serve

8. Family reasons

9. State or local political interference

10. Pressure to raise money, especially a new capital campaign

This research was one of the reasons for viewing presidential succession and transition as a never-ending cycle. The factors that lead boards and presidents to terminate a presidency are usually multiple and interrelated over time. Nancy Axelrod, who once served as a vice president of the Association of Governing Boards, then as the founding chief executive of what is now known as BoardSource, and later as an executive recruiter, says what is seldom seen in print:

> *"The dirty little secret is that a striking number of chief executives depart as a result of unarticulated feuds between themselves and board members. These disagreements can simmer beneath the surface for long periods of time until they are defined with shattering clarity only after the chief executive resigns or is dismissed." (Axelrod, 2002)*

There are other general themes to consider in trying to understand why presidents depart when they do. One approach is to focus on "job fit." The Gallup Organization (Clifton), People Management (Arthur Miller), and others have done useful research on what makes people successful in certain activities and unsuccessful in others. The keys for an institution are to (1) define the kind of president it needs, (2) find people with those characteristics, (3) select one of them, and (4) encourage the new president to accentuate his or her positives and delegate to others some functions that are not strengths. Boards and presidents need to honor this principle. More research in this area and more attention to what we already know in the selection and evaluation of presidents could lead to more successful presidencies. We will address this again in later chapters.

Inadequate communications is another reason many presidencies end prematurely. There are multiple opportunities for miscommunication based on differing assumptions. Boards have difficulty speaking with one voice, and presidents find it impossible to understand or be understood by all the constituents important to the campus. Often, a board chair, the president, or a friendly facilitator can clarify issues and smooth the way for better relationships—and a more satisfying presidency.

A happy circumstance is when the president tells the board, "We have accomplished all the major goals you and I agreed on when I was hired. Now, I am convinced, the environment has changed and the university's needs are different, requiring, in my view at least, a different type of president." Well, the board may disagree. Yet this theme of "my work is done" is fairly common, and a wise board works with these presidents to keep creating new mountains to climb for their incumbent chief executives.

Finally, wise presidents and discerning boards know that any institution goes through cycles, each requiring a different style or set of experiences. While more difficult to pin down, some situations require an institution to find a special kind of president to contend with unique challenges or opportunities such as a merger, extensive physical plant expansion, reengineering the entire curriculum, going international, or whatever.

For the remainder of this book, we will look at many pieces of a complex mosaic that makes up a successful presidency and successful board-president relations.

Chapter 2
When the President Takes the Lead

Presidents leave either because they want to, the board wants them to, or because they die or become incapacitated while in office. All presidents much prefer to control their own departures. Almost every president struggles with the timing of a voluntary departure. Sometimes an attractive offer from another institution solves the dilemma, transferring the problem to the board.

When is it time to leave? The literature suggests that most presidents think ten to 15 years is about the right length in one presidency, though the average is closer to seven years. More presidents who are 55 to 60 years-old think hard about whether to stick it out until retirement or to make one more move before it is too late. The job is exhausting. Teaching, retiring, or taking a nonacademic job that has more reasonable demands runs through a president's mind on many occasions. Yet most agree the academic presidency is the best job they ever had. And most want to leave "at their peak" and just before their boards decide it is time to leave!

Former Tufts University President John A. DiBiaggio suggests that "you may be doing the institution more good by leaving than by staying." He goes on to list many of the reasons presidents leave in his forthright article in *Trusteeship*, "When to Pack It In" (DiBiaggio, 1994).

- When you are no longer effective

- When the need arises to act on principle

- When the institution is approaching a crucial moment in its history

- When the job is no longer fun

- When a new challenge presents itself

There are situations where family health issues or a need to relocate to be nearer an ailing parent are legitimate reasons to resign, if with deep regrets. After all, presidents have private lives, too! In the faith community, there is the matter of calling. Many presidents of religiously affiliated institutions or whose faith is essential to an abundant life take seriously the sense of God's calling and are reluctant to move until they feel released from that call. Even without the faith rationale, it is likely that most presidents accept the unusual opportunity to lead a higher education institution with a sense that they have been called upon by the board because they are uniquely able to fulfill the post.

What are the options for leaving a presidency? This is an important question. In any career change, it is better to run to something new than to run away from one's current situation. Some presidents are uncertain about how well they are doing, so they begin to assume the worst and think of bailing out. That is why annual and periodic comprehensive evaluations by the board are so important. (Chapter 35 has more on this important topic.) Basically, when the president is in a position to take the lead, the options are these:

1. **Retire.** Everyone in higher education, including presidents, thinks of delaying formal retirement past age 65. All of us want to prepare for the eventuality that we might live for quite awhile. And when a president's TIAA-CREF pension portfolio is doing poorly, those additional years with salary and benefits are enticing. But who can a president talk to about that before announcing his or her intention to leave? The fortunate president has a board chair or other trustee in whom he can confide and maybe get a read on how the board might feel about a post-presidency role with the campus. (Chapter 9 has more on this subject.) It is good advice to consult with other close friends, financial advisers, doctors, and family members before deciding to announce a retirement. Making such a decision is a big step. Once that decision is made, the president is in a good position to manage most of the events that follow. Ideally, a president already has helped the board prepare a succession plan long before it is needed and then gives the board adequate formal notice when the date for retirement is set.

2. **Accept a new position.** This is an easier decision, in some ways, because the timing usually affects how the process plays out. But the sleepless nights and second-guessing that occur once a president allows his or her name to be seriously considered for a new job makes the process no less consuming. For the sake of the campus, it is wise to notify the board first, then the whole campus community. Explaining the reasons for moving on is important, allowing the campus to adjust in a positive mood for the difficult steps of transition ahead. A departing president should negotiate with the new employer for a period of several months, if possible, to wrap up campus business. Finishing well is important on every job.

3. **Resign without another job.** Unless they are retiring, few presidents leave without prospects for employment. Yet irreconcilable issues with the board often force such decisions, though they often can be made with a surfeit of emotion and haste. Health issues also may trigger such decisions. Some presidents would take their cabinets into their confidence before making such an announcement. Every president needs an external support group whose love and concern go beyond the job as well as the immediate emotional support of their spouse. Naturally, when a president resigns under these circumstances, the departure date is often within weeks, and there is little control over events once the announcement is made. Boards need to handle these situations with great care or risk significant institutional damage.

For the campus and the board to make a good transition, the ideal situation is for a president to announce a departure at least nine months to one year before leaving. Every president has talked to enough peers and watched friends go through these situations, and all are conscious of what leaving means to the board, campus colleagues, donors, alumni, and others. It is not a decision to make alone. If ever wise counsel was important, this is one of those times.

Chapter 3
When the Board Takes the Lead

"Was he fired, or did he leave voluntarily?" Whenever a vacancy is announced, this question inevitably is among the buzz when people first hear of a departure. The social protocols of the academy often camouflage outright firings. The frequent explanation is that "the parties agreed it was time for a change."

Boards influence the why and the when of presidential changes more than they believe. This book focuses on the continuous cycle of transitions because hundreds of issues surrounding a president and the board can lead one or the other to believe it is time for a change—or perhaps time to negotiate a longer than expected tenure. Some presidents want strong boards and work to see that happen. Other presidents prefer rubber-stamp boards and become frustrated whenever the board wants to flex its muscles.

Every campus abhors a leadership vacuum. Theodore J. Marchese, one of higher education's most thoughtful commentators, observed that "A sudden departure can undermine morale, sever relationships with donors...unsettle internal talent and governance, and put a damper on fund-raising. The board's own morale and standing suffer, too." (Marchese, 2001) We agree. That is why we urge presidents and boards to adopt a transition plan that anticipates most of the following situations:

1. **A sudden resignation.** Most often, this situation occurs when a president accepts another job and cannot give the board much notice. The board and the campus will have mixed reactions. Many such outgoing presidents enjoy the same public displays of gratitude and affection as a long-tenured and much-loved president who retires at age 65. Other sudden resignations will generate feelings of betrayal, especially if only three or four years have passed since the president arrived. Or the reaction could be "Most of us are glad to see him go," in which case the president's wisdom in seeking other employment before the entire board felt the same way is confirmed.

   Whatever the responses to the surprise announcement, the board will need to act decisively and promptly. The board chair must quickly assume the key leadership role on campus to ensure continuity, address morale issues, and serve as the campus spokesman during the transition. An interim or acting president will need to be hired (the next chapter addresses this matter), and a national search eventually will have to be conducted.

2. **Death.** Approximately 3 percent of presidencies end when the incumbent dies in office. How the board reacts depends on whether a long-term illness gave advance warning or whether the death was sudden. Neither is a happy situation, but the campus is much more forgiving and patient than in other scenarios.

    As is the case with a sudden resignation, the board must address short-term and long-term issues of transition. The board chair must assume the lead role but also take extra measures to ensure that the spouse and family are given special attention and care. The departed president's staff also must shoulder an extra load by attending to various unfinished business. None of us expects to die in office, but a worthy exercise might be to leave information and instructions for staff and family in separate "If I should die" files.

3. **Termination.** This prerogative of a board is never easy to do; it is seldom done well; and it almost always is initiated later than it should be. It never is easy because the board meets infrequently, understands only a sliver of the president's life, and usually differs on the circumstances and timing that should lead to terminating a president. All board members should understand the trauma to the institution a forced termination brings. Termination is seldom done well because most boards have no experience with the process; confidentialities are often breached; emotions are high; and there are few opportunities for civil discussion among the parties before the decision is made. For all of these reasons, most boards that must make this difficult decision do so a year or more after "the writing was on the wall."

    Again, the board chair is the most critical actor in facilitating appropriate board dialogue, with the president and with trustees, once the board is aware of serious issues. Sometimes it is a "no confidence" vote of the faculty that provides the wake-up call. Other times it is growing discontent among board members over time. In some cases, the president's relations with the board chair never clicked, and too little trust developed. In this regard, recently fired presidents can be naïve.

    There is no difference of opinion between the president and the board when some public indiscretion leaves everyone in absolute agreement that "this president has to go." Thankfully, higher education leaders seldom are involved in criminal acts or major financial or moral indiscretions. Yet every board chair should think about the "what if" questions surrounding worst case scenarios.

4. **Board-initiated mutual agreements.** Boards and presidents can have differing assumptions about when between the ages 62 and 70 might be a good time to leave. Boards might initiate the discussion through an annual performance review, or a board chair, reflecting an informal consensus of the board, might choose any day of the week to bring up the subject.

As you can imagine, when the tough issues are brought to a head by the board, the president and his family are thrown into emotional turmoil. Why now? What is behind this? Haven't I been doing a good job? Should I resign now? Do I have any rights? These feelings can not be eliminated entirely, but a good board should adopt a succession and transition plan that suggests when and how these discussions should take place.

Because these situations are not entirely performance-based, there is little time to work out privately a planned resignation with plenty of notice. The board can ensure, in spite of the difficulties that might emerge within the president's family, that the president is appropriately honored with a dignified celebration of service.

Much more could be said about these four categories of departure when the board takes the lead. Each contains many variations, but the theme is: Be prepared. As Stanley M. Gault, a former chair of the College of Wooster (Ohio), has said, "The board must act in a way that is visible and expeditious. The board must show that it is responsible. It must inspire confidence, whatever actions it takes." (Footlick, 2002) And, we would add, boards don't do this easily unless they are blessed with a chair who leads them to fulfill this good advice.

Chapter 4
Acting and Interim Presidents

Many astute observers believe private colleges should give more thought to "rent a president" strategies. Interested? The words interim and acting are sometimes used interchangeably. But there is a distinction with a difference. First, the easy one.

Acting presidents usually are designated by sitting presidents, with or without board consultation, to be "in charge" when the president is on a trip or temporarily incapacitated by illness. It is good practice for everyone to know that when the president is not on campus, this person will make a decision should a need arise. Unless the absence is for several weeks or months, the acting president usually would not move into the presidential office space. The most natural individuals to have this designation are the executive vice president, provost, or another experienced vice president.

Ordinarily, this "designated leader" does not think much about the role and does not anticipate using such short-lived authority to do anything drastic. Maybe sign a document. Probably chair a cabinet meeting. Perhaps stand in for the president at a ceremonial or public event. It is wise for the president to develop a memorandum that lays out expectations and anticipates possible needs for significant actions. Since September 11, 2001, campus crisis-management plans are a legitimate priority. The acting president must be aware of matters related to health, safety, legal responsibilities, and unique emergency actions that are the responsibility of whoever wears the mantle of chief executive for that day.

In the event of a president's illness, what might start out short term could extend for months. In such a case, the board should be brought into decisions about timing, the added workload of the acting president, and the prospects for needing a longer term interim or acting president.

Interim presidents, on the other hand, are the "only CEO" during a period of campus life. Mary Everley offers a useful definition of "interim president" in a 1996 *Trusteeship* article, "Supporting an Interim President":

> *"An individual so designated by the trustees...and given the responsibilities and authority of the presidency in the period between the departure of one president and the assumption of office by another, or during periods of an incumbent president's extended absence." (Everley, 1996)*

The normal "extended absence" might be a well-deserved presidential sabbatical or an extended illness that started out with the help of an "acting" president but develops into the prospect of several more months, with the hope that the "real" president can return. At this point the board usually takes more ownership of the decisions.

As Everley defines the role, however, the need is for someone to occupy the president's office and full duties for a period of time, normally anywhere from three months to a year, although some interim presidents have been known to serve several years in rare situations.

Many private colleges underestimate the value of bringing in an interim president between presidencies. Too often a search for a "permanent" president is rushed when the board finds itself with an unanticipated departure. There is no time for a careful assessment of where the college is and should be heading. A rushed search can be a short-term solution and a long-term mistake. But even when the college has time for a "normal" search, there can be good arguments for selecting an interim president.

The Association of Governing Boards of Universities and Colleges (AGB) in 1995 published a complete and helpful study, "The Interim Presidency: Guidelines for University and College Governing Boards," by E. K. Fretwell, Jr. The study included interviews with 52 interim presidents in 20 states, 16 of whom were serving independent colleges. Any campus contemplating an interim presidency will find Fretwell's study useful.

Drawing on this 50-page report, here are the key steps for a board of trustees:

1. **Decide whether to pursue an interim.** Are there special reasons to delay the search for a permanent president? Do you want someone just to maintain things for a season or to accomplish specific goals best done before a new president is found? Given the way the former president served and exited, what kind of interim would best fit the situation? If the decision is to move ahead with a search and selection of an interim for, say, one year, then the board also might need to designate someone as acting president until that task is accomplished.

2. **Search for the interim.** It could be someone on campus or an experienced person from the outside. Use a small search committee able to move quickly. Tap consultants, former presidents of similar institutions, national associations, trustees, and others for names. Select someone able to begin almost immediately. Normally, make clear that the interim will not be a candidate during the presidential search. Consult with faculty and others before making the selection.

3. **Negotiate a clear employment agreement.** Agree on expectations, reporting arrangements, the role of the spouse, and other things important to a successful interim presidency. Pay the person what you would pay a new president and expect full-time work, perhaps accommodating the interim's need to return periodically to his or her home base.

4. **Treat the interim as the chief executive officer.** Expect regular board reports on agreed-upon goals. Ensure the cabinet, faculty, and staff understand the goals and any special limitations the board has established for this new "temp." The interim may see difficult personnel decisions that should be made now to enhance a good start for the eventual holder of the office. The board chair and perhaps a couple other trustees should meet regularly with the interim to discuss these kinds of lasting decisions. In public, this person should have the title "president," without the interim designation, as the length of service may be somewhat open.

5. **Proceed with a careful search for next president.** This process may wisely be delayed until the interim can help the board assess the leadership challenges for the next five to ten years (see Chapters 11-21).

The AGB report includes advice to potential interim presidents from those who have served in that position. Again, only some highlights are needed here:

1. **Be honest about your interest and abilities.** Not all temperaments can adapt well to temporary assignments. Would an interim presidency mid-career enhance or detract from your career goals? How would moving for a short time affect family and professional relationships? What type of campus, facing what kinds of challenges, would interest you most?

2. **Investigate each situation carefully.** When you are approached about serving as an interim president, take time (you may have only a few days) to investigate as much as possible. For any campus looking for an interim president, there normally are several not-so-normal dynamics. Read public information, but ask friends and campus contacts how to eliminate some of the surprises should you accept an appointment. Is the board clear on what it wants? Are the time frames appropriate for your situation? Are your personality and talents a good fit for this situation?

3. **Negotiate the employment agreement.** This may be the first time this board has ever thought about employing an interim. It may be your first time! So take the few days necessary for both you and the board to feel you have mutual understandings on duties, compensation, length of service, spousal responsibilities, and so forth.

4. **Start off right.** Depending on the situation, you may need to move quickly to allay fears, help move the campus into some stage of functionality, and regain good morale. Some healing often is required. Get acquainted with all the key players fast. Create times to meet key campus groups, community leaders, and major donors. Listen a lot!

5. **Adjust to the situation.** No matter how much investigation you did before accepting the post, there will be surprises. Keep in close touch with the board chair when significant decisions seem necessary. Involve people who will need to live with the decision after you are gone. You may need to make a key administrative appointment, but most of those are best left for the next president. Usually, finances are or become an issue during an interim presidency. Help clarify administrative roles, define reality, stay close to the numbers, and provide moral and spiritual leadership as the needs suggest.

6. **Connect with the former president.** You may be the catalyst for reconciliation if the former president died, left for another job suddenly, or resigned under unhappy circumstances. It helps no one to allow unhealthy relationships and attitudes to persist for too long.

7. **Help find and prepare for your successor.** The board may not invite you to help in their search for a new president. Yet you will see and hear things important to the search committee. Offer your help, but honor the board's decision on what that might or might not include. In the meantime, you can "make lists" of things you do and things you notice that will help the new president. Keep the budget process and other cyclical tasks on schedule.

8. **Say your goodbyes.** You will build some relationships and loyalties within a few months that may be difficult to let go. Remember that you were hired as a temporary leader; don't expect a lot of ceremony when it is time to leave. The campus needs to focus on another major transition when the name of the new president is announced.

Departing with Style

Chapter 5
The Incumbent's Choices

The decision has been made. The board knows you are leaving. Now what?

The outgoing president's choices at this point have all to do with the circumstances. Many others will have ideas about how you should say your good-byes. Some will occur at official events, others at more informal occasions. Some will be fun, others awkward, and a few downright embarrassing. You do have choices! You and your family should think about this in advance and make your preferences known.

When You Retire

This is the best of circumstances. Everyone has known for many months that your last full-time position is coming to an end (or so you all think). The campus is focused on the work of the search committee, and your colleagues have adjusted emotionally to the fact that you are leaving. You have been winding up your work, and your family has been looking for new housing, anticipating the future. Here are some suggestions and observations from those who have been through this period:

1. Professionally, be realistic about what you can accomplish as a lame duck. Pick a few priorities you are sure will serve the campus well and accomplish them before your successor arrives.

2. Name a well-respected person on campus to serve as your transition coordinator. Alert this person to your preferences for dinners, awards, fundraising events, gifts, and so forth. Recognize that your campus colleagues will also want to do some things important to them, as well.

3. Suggest to the board chair that a transition committee be named to work with you in anticipating the arrival of a new president. This committee might consist of a cabinet officer, faculty leader, someone from the business office, your executive assistant, and perhaps a community representative. One task of such a committee is to determine which documents should be ready to give to the new president right after appointment (in addition to the considerable amount of information the finalists will receive as part of the search process).

4. Major donors will appreciate a special visit from you to reminisce, to receive your deep appreciation, and to hear you express the hope that they will continue to support the college.

5. Anticipate what might help your successor in terms of housing and office space. Perhaps you should facilitate some upgrades that could be done on your watch (short of picking out window treatments and wallpaper).

When You Resign

If your resignation comes as a surprise, it usually means you have taken another position. Naturally, the dynamics of this situation are different. You wake up each morning with ideas for your new position. You have little time to find housing at the new location and already have begun to read materials to prepare you for your new responsibilities. Yet you want to finish strong on this campus. Some of the above list may apply, but these may be additional suggestions to consider:

1. Board members and cabinet officers will appreciate a personal conversation with you so they can understand your reasons for leaving.

2. Members of the news media also will be curious about your reasons for leaving, and you'll want to allow time soon after your announcement for interviews. Assuming your departure is truly voluntary, you can be generous with your praise for the campus as well as your rationale for taking another assignment.

3. The same applies to alumni. A special mailing or a lengthy print interview in the next alumni magazine will be important.

When You Leave Under a Cloud

Whether you chose to resign "as a matter of principle," or "for personal reasons," or because of "significant differences in philosophy with the board," or were actually fired (hard, but not the end of the world), the unique circumstances dictate more limited choices in your effort to depart gracefully. These observations may stimulate your thinking, knowing that they have limited value if you have been terminated in a surprise decision by your board.

1. Work to maintain good communications with the board chair, even if the relationship is strained. It will save you and the campus much grief. Be gracious whenever you can. You won't win and the campus won't win if you go on the defensive. Few words, or no words, are often the best course.

2. If you technically make the choice to leave (and most boards will give you the option of resigning before having to fire you), give yourself a couple weeks to leave your office in good shape. It may not be possible, but it gives you a chance to say some good-byes, brief people on what needs follow-up, show that you are not leaving in a huff, and write letters to key people explaining the situation in the best light. After all, some healing will be necessary, and you may want to be invited back to campus someday.

3. Consider the need for immediate legal advice on some matters relating to your employment agreement. Counseling for you and your family also might be wise.

4. Think of your family first. Tell your true story. If you need to apologize for some things, do so. Ask forgiveness. Too many fallen leaders become defensive or vindictive. It's not the way to go out.

Strengthening Your Legacy

Although some colleagues may object to your efforts to shape your own legacy, you should attend to any initiatives that were passionate priorities, documenting changes that have proved successful. Honor those whose work should be recognized and whose labors will continue to embed your vision into the fabric of the institution. This task should not be an obsession, but a worthy focus in your remaining days.

To retire happy, loved, respected, and at the right time is every person's dream. But we know that happens for only about half of all presidents. To leave early so you can do something you might love even more is not a bad alternative. But even when you think things are going well, situations can change dramatically. Always seek wise counsel before acting on instincts and emotions. Keep open communications with your board chair. Never compromise your own integrity. Others may be able to speak the truth in love better than you. When the time comes to leave, know that the sun will rise again in the morning.

Chapter 6
The Community's Needs

The wishes of many people need to be considered in any presidential transition. Depending on the circumstances, you, as president, may assume a good deal or very little of the leadership necessary to allow the community to make the transition. For the community, helping you depart with style and grace is extremely important. The community's perception of how leadership change is managed sends a message to everyone affiliated with the institution.

The community's needs differ depending on the reasons for your departure. Consider three scenarios:

First, the happy occasion when you announce your own retirement. This is normally discussed with the board a year in advance. A few people may be surprised by the announcement, and some people will begin to think of good ways to celebrate your service. There may be an awkward period when no one seems in charge. The board chair often is the most appropriate person to assume leadership in appointing a committee of a few trustees, key administrators, and others to monitor the campus calendar and serve as a coordinating committee of sorts. You and your family often have preferences that should be integrated into the planning. You will want to host some events yourself, but other celebrations would be presumptuous for you to initiate.

Once a retirement date is announced, you should look at the calendar and plan to honor those who have served the campus during your tenure. Your personal style will dictate how this occurs, but celebrations are definitely in order. This changing of the guard is a community experience, and the college or university can gain visibility and credibility by carrying this out well.

The second scenario is when a president resigns unexpectedly, often to accept another job. If this is your situation, emotions will be mixed, and many will never know the real reasons for your decision. Speculation runs rampant. You begin an intense period of trying to attend to personal and campus priorities while responding to the needs of your future employer.

Again, the board chair would do well to convene the president's team and others to explore the time frame, the circumstances of the departure, the president's wishes, forthcoming campus events that might be used to acknowledge the president's contributions, resources available for the transition, and so forth. Of course, the board also must focus on conducting a search, perhaps with less than the desired nine to 12 months notice.

A modification of this scenario is when a president has tenure or has expressed a desire to resume teaching at the same university. This is best discussed privately with board leaders well in advance. This can be a welcome or a sad transition, often reflected in differing opinions on campus. When a president hopes to remain on campus, the transition likely will be less in the realm of a public event and geared more toward quiet acknowledgements in community gatherings. Together, the board and the president must clarify what role is expected once the presidential duties are completed.

Another modification occurs when a president becomes severely disabled or dies in office. The well-prepared board moves immediately to implement policies that were in place prior to such a crisis (see Chapter 12). An interim president is named, a search committee is convened, someone is appointed to help the family, legal and medical advice is sought, and appropriate gatherings are planned. This is when a board chair earns his or her stripes.

Undoubtedly the most difficult scenario for the community is when the board and president must announce a resignation that everyone knows is forced. Terminating a president is extremely difficult for any board, but trustees periodically must make such decisions for the sake of the community.

The board chair is crucial behind the scenes prior to and immediately following a forced departure. Explaining the departure (is it a retirement or resignation?) establishes a tone for the future. A removal, without tact and compassion, can lead to a situation where damage control becomes the order of the day. Public statements portraying divisions among trustees, faculty, and students on reasons for the president's departure should be avoided at all costs. Above all, every statement the board chair makes on behalf of the institution must be factual and truthful.

A president who is terminated but needs or agrees to stay in the area for several months may be given access to the president's office, offered assistance in communications, and in some cases, even allowed to use the presidential title until the official time of departure. Normally, a president in this situation will refrain from being present at campus events or becoming involved in campus issues. Again, the chair should facilitate these decisions.

Each vice president also must communicate appropriately with various campus constituencies. This is no time to bad-mouth a departing president but to demonstrate that campus leaders are on top of the situation.

In summary, this is an all-too-brief alert to the lasting effects of a poorly handled presidential transition on internal and external constituents. To ignore this set of decisions and actions can be very costly to the institution's well-being.

Chapter 7
The Board's Role

There is no departing with style without the board chair's active leadership. It is likely that several trustees were recruited with the help of the departing president and, depending on the circumstances, will want to do something appropriate. But two dozen or more trustees acting on their own can contribute to chaos rather than a thoughtful and dignified departure. Likewise, the president recruited many administrators, and as soon as a departure is announced, they will start thinking of ways to mark the upcoming transition. The chair must evince strong and immediate leadership with the board and should help administrators coordinate campus plans for the departing president.

The board's actions at this time convey important messages to the campus, to the outgoing president and family, and to finalists in the search process. These candidates will be talking to the departing president before and after the final selection. In attempting to manage the transition effectively, the board has four sets of decisions relating to the departure of a president, all influenced greatly by the reasons for the transition.

1. **How to celebrate the contributions of the outgoing president.** The circumstances of the departure will dictate how much or little celebration should be planned. The board chair should appoint a small task force of trustees to consider how the board should express its appreciation; this usually is done at the last board meeting with the outgoing president. The chair also might work with the provost or executive vice president to appoint a campus-wide committee to work on all other celebrations. The board should be generous in its expressions of thanks, regardless of the circumstances of the departure.

   Here are a few common board initiatives:

   • Have a board-sponsored banquet a few weeks before the formal departure. This event needs adequate notice, a good committee of staff, a budget, an invitation list of major constituents, and so forth.

   • Commission a work of art, name a building after the president, sponsor a lecture series around the departing president's passion, confer an honorary doctorate on the president and spouse, organize an album of letters from key people, produce a video.

- Sponsor a campus convocation where trustees, faculty, staff, and students see the departing president "pass the baton" of leadership to the incoming president. Ideally, everyone will see that a friendship has been formed and that each leader respects the other.

- Invite the outgoing president to confer with the board's executive committee about family needs. These may relate to such matters as housing costs, ownership of certain household goods that may be in question because of who paid for them, expenses of moving to a new location, and completion of college for any children receiving tuition waivers. Be generous! The goodwill and the model this provides will pay dividends for a long time.

2. **How to compensate a departing president.** There are no common principles here. Some boards keep a president on the payroll until the last day, provide a nicely wrapped gift, and leave it at that. Some approve a generous severance gift of cash, a new car, or some other substantive reward for good service. It is wise to allow occupancy of the campus home as long as possible and to help cover moving costs, because that honors the whole community and reflects generosity. Some boards offer continued compensation for a role as consultant to the incoming president, whether for the value of the anticipated consultations to the new president or as an appropriate rationale for being generous for excellent past service. Other boards fund a well-deserved sabbatical.

   When the compensation could be substantial, a wise board moves quickly upon knowledge of a future transition to put a reserve fund in the budget prior to naming a new president. This might even be spread over two budget cycles, but it removes from the plate of the next president what could be a sensitive issue.

3. **What title to confer on an outgoing president.** There may be a tradition or protocol about conferring titles on former presidents at some campuses, often linked to the president's length of service. When a president has added great value to the life and growth of a campus, and is not moving to another presidency, the title "president emeritus" is appropriate. It is possible, after an appropriate interval, that a president emeritus can be helpful to a campus, particularly with major donors who have special affection for the president.

   The question of naming an outgoing president to the post of chancellor upon retirement from a successful presidency is a special issue that is explored in Chapter 9.

4. **How to facilitate the physical departure.** It is always surprising to hear of misunderstandings about, or lack of attention to, some practical issues of departing presidents. The board chair and/or executive committee should meet with the president soon after the decision to depart is made. Matters to discuss might include use of the president's home, time for the campus to redecorate for the incoming family, tuition waivers for the president's children, ownership of gifts given to the president such as art or books, access to the president's assistant for help in moving plans, unused vacation time, and so forth. All outgoing presidents and their spouses have issues that no one but the board can resolve.

These reminders for the board can get lost in the board's essential work of finding the next president. Perhaps while a search committee is at work on that task, a transition committee could be appointed both to help the outgoing president depart with style and to anticipate the needs of an incoming president.

Chapter 8
The Family's Needs

The families of presidents often are overlooked in transitions. The focus is on the president, as it should be. But spouses and children also are thrust into life changes that need attention. Their physical and emotional needs can be even greater than the person leaving the job. Presidents, you are their first line of support. Board chairs, you need to keep the family high on your list of concerns as well.

As is true of so many transitions, the circumstances make all the difference. In surprise departures, the family suffers most. In happy retirements, the family has been part of the planning and is much better prepared.

Presidents usually are focused on the work and challenges at hand. They can become so immersed in the tasks of transition, particularly if these include preparing for another leadership role, that they may suppress their own emotions and fail to recognize others' emotional needs. Spouses and children may feel ignored and frustrated during these periods. Naturally, family needs vary depending on the ages of any children at home, their schooling, outside employment or key volunteer roles of the spouse, specific health issues, and so forth. But all face the difficulty of leaving friends and facing the unknown.

This is a time when the family needs support from friends and colleagues. Sometimes those people are just there. They assume responsibility without any institutional initiative. If this is not the case, board chairs might offer to recruit a small group of people to work with the presidential spouse and/or children to help with issues of their own transition. (Few families will ask.) Once begun, this little "committee" can monitor needs and take helpful and supportive action. Here is a starter checklist of possible areas for attention:

- Help with moving arrangements and packing, including who pays for what

- Arrange for special events for the family to say thank you and goodbye

- Facilitate special arrangements for the children to complete school activities

- Consider offering future tuition assistance to children or grandchildren

- Come to agreement on which items belong to the family or to the institution

- Facilitate a meeting between the outgoing family and the incoming family

- Coordinate repairs to or major renovation of the president's home

- Recognize that the spouse's job is also ending when a move is planned

- Provide for some part-time or volunteer help

- Identify needs for family counseling, job-placement assistance, or financial services

It is difficult to anticipate the many ways a family might need or appreciate help. Again, the way the campus treats the outgoing presidential family will not be lost on others, particularly the incoming president's family. A little extra love and care go a long way in this regard.

Chapter 9
The Possibility of a Chancellorship

Many boards fear the unknown. They are concerned about who will replace the current successful president who plans to retire. They want to be certain major donors stay loyal when the president leaves. Someone is likely to float the idea of engaging the outgoing president part-time as a chancellor.

The idea might come from the president himself. He has known colleagues who have received half or more pay for such service. Sometimes an office and secretarial assistance come with the job. Perhaps medical benefits or a car. Maybe a chancellorship makes sense for both the outgoing president and the campus.

Perhaps—but it doesn't often work well. Here are the problems that frequently occur when the board engages an outgoing president to be chancellor:

1. Most people ready to be president neither need nor want their predecessor's help (except in rare occurrences), and they would prefer to ask for the help on their own terms. This applies even to work with major donors. Former presidents might continue their personal friendships with some major donors (interestingly, however, this is rare), but those donors want to meet the new president and may even prefer to receive the first call from the new president rather than his or her predecessor. Some joint donor visits to pass the baton can be helpful.

2. When a board drafts a job description for its chancellor-to-be, most people of conscience want to fulfill it, and will go the extra mile to earn the pay that goes with it. Frequently, however, the new president is not comfortable with the job description, particularly after the first several months, but is still too new to campus to want to complain. But the added stress and distraction take their toll.

3. Many trustees, faculty, administrators, media representatives, and donors have excellent relationships with the outgoing president, and some may be tempted to take their needs to the chancellor rather than "bother" the new president. The potential for problems is obvious.

4. Some former presidents think they can disengage from the day-to-day operational issues when they move to a part-time (or full-time) chancellorship, only to discover they cannot. The temptation to "help out" the rookie replacement is too much. They begin to offer advice to long-standing colleagues, and even make a suggestion or two about the new president to a few friendly trustees. Disaster in the making.

5. Very rarely do a chancellor and a new president "click" and become mutually reinforcing friends. Both like to be in charge; both want to make decisions that affect the campus. One inevitably becomes a competitor to the other, and bad things result.

6. Periodically, the financial commitment made by the board to the chancellor all of a sudden prevents some other priorities from getting funded.

A private college should not risk these potential problems. In a real sense, "the college is not big enough" for the old and the new presidents.

Does the research corroborate these conclusions? John W. Moore and Joanne M. Burrows surveyed state college and university presidents (Moore, 2001) and included this comment before saying there needs to be more research on this important question:

> "This study confirms the conventional wisdom that former presidents and their successors benefit from extended social distance. Experience also seems to support this long-held point of view. However, the authors are intrigued by situations revealed in this study in which the relationships between predecessors and successors were characterized by frequent contact, mutual support, and continued contributions by former presidents not only for the benefit of the institution but also of the successor."

Of course there are exceptions to all generalizations. A few rare personalities have that non-threatening, gracious way about them. They are available when the new president calls upon them, and they are able to stay away the rest of the time. They can "just say no" when others try to involve them in things that should go to the chief executive, and they realize that the board needs just one agent to implement its policies, not a shadow leader playing back-up or alternate. Occasionally, a departing president is asked to serve on the board of trustees, but the results are mixed.

How to predict whether a president-chancellor relationship will work out well is the task. Here are some suggestions to ensure more success than failure:

1. During the search, ask whether the retiring president would be available to serve the institution in some special, defined ways after retirement. If so, ask whether that option could be discussed with the finalists in the search.

2. Assure the finalists that, should they so choose, the board would support their decision to engage the former president as "special assistant" or "senior adviser" or whatever title the two of them agree to. The board could even put enough money in a reserve account to make it easy for such an arrangement to take place.

3. In this scenario, it might be possible to announce a chancellorship that is mutually designed at the time the board announces a new president, or at the time the campus meets the new president.

4. If a board is determined to name the retiring president chancellor, some of the details of the assignment will need to be worked out between the new president and the chancellor. Maybe not salary, but surely such matters as office space and help, assignments, attendance at board meetings, and roles on any campus-related groups or organizations should be the call of the new president.

To be sure, there are some excellent president-chancellor relationships. Sadly, however, there are more stories of presidents leaving early, presidents being terminated, and open conflicts affecting the whole campus—all because a board and/or outgoing president presumed to know what was best for a campus. If you go down this road, drive carefully.

Chapter 10
Life After the Presidency

We have some advice for you who are departing a presidency. Whether you retire from full-time work, move on to another presidency (remember that one report says 20 percent do so), leave for another leadership role, or are terminated by the board (the same report says this happens to 15 percent of presidents), life goes on. (Moore, 2001) The degree to which you defined yourself by the title and role of president affects how you adjust the day after giving up the reins to your successor.

The following might be helpful reference points or reminders for thinking of the future:

1. If married, keep communications open and move forward as a team.

2. Send heart-felt notes and letters of thanks to all who served you well and helped you achieve during your presidency.

3. Forgive and forget those incidents that no longer are important. Lingering anger or regret can hinder your next chapter. Realize that some emotional scars will stay with you, but look ahead not behind.

4. Pick up on those hobbies, neglected relationships, places you have always wanted to visit, and books you have put off reading. Schedule your days and weeks at a more reasonable pace to acknowledge that you have been a focused "doer" for so long you have neglected just "being" the person you want to be.

5. Offer to be available to your successor, whether through a formal consulting agreement or as an informal source of wise counsel. Have a "you call me, I'll not call you" arrangement with your successor. "Don't interfere" is the common rule.

6. Don't be offended if you receive fewer calls than you might expect from former colleagues, but do stay in touch with those who became good friends, while not "snooping" about campus life.

7. Even if you want another full-time job, a planned sabbatical of three to six months may be the nicest gift you could ever arrange for yourself. Maybe longer.

8. Reflect on what you did and what you learned during your presidency. Write it down to help you clarify things. More than a few presidents have written a cathartic book that also was helpful to those coming behind.

9. Write thank-you notes to major donors who were there when you needed them, not to suggest that you still represent the campus but only to express gratitude. This will leave them open to overtures from your successor.

10. Get another physical, visit with a nutritionist, review your financial plan and estate plan with an expert, and bring your personal matters up to date.

11. Recognize that your emotional and spiritual bearings may need attention. Your spouse, children, and grandchildren deserve you at your best. Plan more time with them.

12. Always speak highly of your successor. Never berate trustees or colleagues. It doesn't improve things and could hinder your legacy.

13. Find someone to mentor. It could be a graduate student, a young faculty member, or an aspiring college administrator. This can be one of the most mutually rewarding experiences.

14. Consider immersing yourself once again into your academic discipline.

15. Consider moving from the community to create a new home base and to reduce the appearance of staying too close to people and decisions on campus. If you are motivated to do so, consider remodeling a new home as a good outlet for your energy.

A number of former presidents who shared an affiliation during their presidency choose to gather as couples or singles from time to time. The job ends, but good relationships continue. Although you will have special relationships with some of your former trustees, beware that ongoing friendships with them will be threatening to your successor.

If you go on to other types of service, whether in government, the professions, or business, you will find that the presidency was an uncommon preparation. After all, you played every dimension of the roles played by corporate CEOs, mayors, political leaders, pastors, and others who carry important mantles of leadership.

Some presidents find that their most rewarding years are after retirement. Former academic leaders who find fulfilling work as volunteers, consultants, board members, authors, and in other roles for as long as their health allows offer inspiration. Of course, this is also the time to discover more balance, rest, and leisure. Whatever path you choose, be sure it adds meaning and purpose to your life and that of your family.

Searching Successfully

Chapter 11
Preparing to Be a Candidate

Some presidents think it is almost futile to "plan" to be a president, while others say that making wise choices along the way puts you in better stead than someone who doesn't give it a thought. To be sure, presidents with both of these outlooks are serving with distinction today.

Graduate School

Any aspiring college president today should opt for a doctorate, preferably the Ph.D. That's the "gold card" for admission to most presidencies. The 2002 edition of "The American College President" points out that 56 percent of college and university presidents had earned Ph.D.s and 21 percent Ed.D.s. Interestingly, 44 percent had their highest degree in the field of higher education, followed by 14 percent in each of the social sciences and the humanities.

While some new presidents do not have terminal degrees, it is safe to assume that this will become rarer. The field in which you achieve such a degree should be guided by your interests, not by what someone else suggests.

Once Your Career is Launched

If you are an aspiring president, the following suggestions might help you realize your ambitions:

1. Join professional associations and societies whose meetings, publications, and networking opportunities expose you to issues and trends throughout the academy.

2. Evaluate your strengths and abilities to see whether they match your understanding of the common characteristics of presidents. Do you possess high energy, the ability to assume responsibility and make difficult decisions, the capacity to engage others in the deliberative process of campus decision-making, an interest in communicating vision and strategic goals?

3. Seek mentors who model for you the best aspects of academic leadership.

4. Read books and journal articles about the academic presidency.

5. Volunteer for committees and task forces that give you insights into how and why campuses work well or not so well.

6. Allow yourself to be active in a search—even before you are sure you are ready—to learn how the search is conducted. Your mind and emotions will take you places you didn't know existed until you looked a presidency square in the eye.

7. Seek out fund-raising experiences.

8. Serve on a board of trustees or try to observe the workings of a college board.

9. Stay in good physical shape; it is important to demonstrate stamina in these jobs.

When a Vacancy Appeals to You

The common wisdom is that it is best to be sought for a position, not to seek one. In other words, it is better if someone nominates you and the search committee calls you. Every vacancy is advertised, and every search has applicants. But you might want to discuss your interest with others who would be in a good position to pass along your name.

Once you know your name is in the hopper, it behooves you to research the campus. Explore its Web site, study the search materials, talk to people who know the campus well, study its history and campus culture. Learn as much as you can about the financial status of the institution and its last accreditation report.

If you are a sitting president, you know that being identified as interested in another job entails significant risks. Most presidents ask for confidentiality, at least until they hear, "If the job were offered to you, would you be inclined to accept?" When a search committee is willing to pose that question, they are likely to want to talk to some of your board members and executive colleagues. Naturally, you'll want to alert them beforehand as to what is going on.

If you are under active consideration by a search committee, this is the time to confide in your spouse and family and in a few trusted friends. There will be many personal decisions throughout the process that will benefit from wise counsel.

In sum, it is appropriate to make choices that are more rather than less likely to prepare you to be a president. While the road to the president's office is not often laid out clearly on a map, those who are the "lucky" ones tend to be those who are prepared. Be sure the substance, not just the prestige, of the job fits your make-up.

Chapter 12
Campus Preparations

Not all presidencies end with a happy retirement. Surprises happen. Vacancies can pop up over night. Is the board prepared? A divided board, working under the emotions surrounding a sudden departure, hurts everyone, including those who will soon be considered presidential candidates. Candidates will ask probing questions and search for the truth about why the president left. One should expect that candidates will do extensive research and will want to discuss matters with the departing president and key campus constituents. The board must be prepared with credible answers.

The longer it takes to conduct a good search, the more difficult it becomes for an institution to recover and gain confidence in itself. Where there is considerable acrimony associated with a parting of the ways, the healing process can be time consuming. Restoration of institutional confidence becomes the most essential aspect of regaining needed trust. An institution moves forward only when a majority of the campus community determines to provide constructive support.

The Board's Role

Whenever a vacancy occurs, a board must be ready. It should have an action plan on file, even years before it might be necessary. The chair should be prepared to act within hours of a presidential resignation. Here are some questions a board will need to consider in formulating a transition plan:

1. How is an acting or interim president selected if needed?

2. Is that person eligible to be a candidate?

3. Should there be a search committee plus a selection committee, or one committee to do both?

4. How many people and how many groups should be represented on the committee?

5. Who should be the appointing authority? (Does the faculty appoint its own representatives or nominate someone to the board?)

6. Who will chair the search committee?

7. Will a search firm be retained and, if so, how and by whom?

8. Alternatively, will a search consultant be used to help the committee do much of the work?

9. What is the budget for a search?

10. Who will provide the staff support for a search?

11. Who must be notified and invited to nominate candidates?

12. What are the essential criteria for selecting a president?

13. What should be the type of on-campus visits by candidates?

14. What should be the type of recommendation back to the board? Should candidates be rank ordered, or should only one favorite be presented?

15. What transition issues concern the board?

16. Who will negotiate the new president's compensation package?

17. How will we ensure the outgoing president is treated fairly?

18. How will we organize a welcome committee to assist the new president and spouse?

19. How will we develop a plan for evaluating the search process to benefit future searches?

Some boards craft a policy that gives immediate authority to the chair to move ahead on appointments, announcements, and so forth. Several good publications on presidential searches appear in the reference section of this book.

A President's Confidential Memorandum

No trustee can imagine all the details that go with the job of president. Boards should consider assigning the task to their presidents of writing an "If I Should Leave or Die" memorandum. This might include essential background on continuing projects, insights into key trustees or major donors that a president would want a successor to know about, priorities that only the chief executive can implement, and so forth. Like the board transition plan, this memorandum should be reviewed annually by the president and filed where someone knows where to find it. These few pages of notes may save the campus considerable time and effort if an acting or interim president can have the predecessor's views on important things to do during a transition. Many presidents have "deals in the works" that perhaps only a successor should know about or be able to complete.

Chapter 13
Board and Search Committee Leadership

No campus figure or outside agency will do the work required of trustees in a presidential transition. While pressure will be great to move quickly, the process must be handled with great wisdom following adequate consultation and deliberation. The wise board, upon notice that a new president is needed, will normally go through this sequence:

1. Respond to immediate family and campus needs if a death is involved. These can be considerable and must reflect the highest level of care and concern.

2. Decide on an acting president if that is what is required. A well-prepared board will have discussed whether it might have to make this choice and knows in advance whether such a person will serve a few days or several weeks.

3. Deliberate on the benefits of an interim president to give adequate time for a search or to provide the campus a time of healing or planning before selecting a permanent chief executive. The circumstances of the former president's departure will often influence this decision. As outlined in Chapter 4, a short search often is required to find the right person for this temporary leader.

4. Review the transition plans or quickly seek help from consultants, search firms, or other presidents. (The list in Chapter 12 might be helpful.)

5. Activate a search committee with clear roles and responsibilities.

Choosing Without a Search Committee

Some campuses may have a succession plan in place that identifies the next president before a vacancy is known, although this is rare. This person could be an executive vice president, a provost, or another senior administrator who has been tapped by the board. Succession plans work best when there is a planned retirement. Although many faculty, alumni, and donors may push for a formal search, choosing a new president without a formal search should not necessarily be discounted, especially in unusual situations. Corporations do it routinely. Small colleges, however, seldom have the attraction for potential chief executives to come a year or two early to learn the ropes.

Boards may also meet at the time a search begins and decide then that there is a well-liked and successful vice president who would make an excellent president. Perhaps that person is critical to a capital campaign or a curriculum revision. It makes sense. Still, many on campus will want that person to compete for the job through a search process. The board must listen to all points of view and then make a wise judgment whether selection without a search is a wise option.

Searching Without a Search Committee

While the average size of a private college's board is about 30, some private colleges with smaller boards may decide the board can function as the search committee. Ordinarily, however, it is wise for search committees to include representatives of the entire campus community. What's more, not all board members have the time or interest to work hard on a search, and the full board should act as an independent evaluator of finalists that another group has identified.

The Ideal Search Committee

There is no consensus on the ideal size or composition of a search committee, but the following suggestions may be valuable:

- Seven to 13 is a good range.

- Trustees should make up one more than half the membership.

- Faculty should have at least two positions, selected by the faculty organization.

- An organized alumni association should be invited to appoint one member.

- A student leader is usually a good addition.

The search will go best when each major segment on campus feels it is represented and that its representatives were not hand-picked by the board. The board usually, however, lays out the criteria for being selected or appointed to the search committee. For example, members should have time for ten or more meetings; they should be committed to a fair and civil process; and they should promise to maintain strict confidentiality during and after the search.

The charge to the search committee should include the key elements included in the list offered in the previous chapter. The board chair has enough to do during a transition and should appoint another senior trustee to chair the search committee. To handle administrative matters, the incumbent's assistant (or someone else who knows the university and the board and can handle details with confidentiality) should be appointed as the search secretary. The committee's budget should include money for meetings, long-distance and conference calls, candidate and committee travel, printing and mailing, and possible funds to facilitate a good transition once the new president is selected. This is in addition to fees for a search firm.

Chapter 14
Search Firm or Not

Once the board focuses on the tasks involved in a presidential search, one of the big decisions is whether to go it alone or invite a search firm to conduct the search, working with the institution's search committee. It is a key decision.

Good Reasons for Not Retaining a Search Firm

Most institutions these days retain search firms, but some small liberal arts colleges occasionally decide to forego this help. Why?

1. They decided to promote an internal person with appeal.

2. The school is denominational, and the bylaws require that a president be active in the denomination. This makes managing a search easier.

3. Some trustees who were part of the last search suggest help from an outside firm was not that helpful.

4. Paying one-third of the first year's salary (a typical search-firm fee) plus the added travel expenses is not worth the cost.

Good Reasons for Retaining a Search Firm

The board and the campus have so much riding on the board's decision about the next president that doing the search with the best help available is a good practice. Here are the reasons:

1. A search is hard work, requiring daily attention. A search committee of busy volunteers needs the discipline of an outside expert to keep the process moving.

2. A search firm brings best practices in evaluating the needs of the campus, how to promote the job, managing candidates professionally so they stay interested, negotiating a contract, and many other elements of the process.

3. A search firm brings the element of a disinterested participant so the process does not get bogged down in campus or board politics.

4. A search firm should be able to identify good candidates outside the normal network—especially nontraditional candidates.

5. A search firm is likely to conduct better reference checks on potential candidates than inexperienced volunteers—and it maintains confidentiality.

6. A search firm is motivated to do a good job because it works primarily on referrals and usually guarantees that if a president fails to stay for one year it will conduct a new search for no fee.

Choosing a Search Firm

Dozens of search firms specialize in academic searches. A few even specialize in small private colleges, or even in faith-based colleges.

Normally, someone on the board contacts a few search firms by phone, asks for written material to review, then recommends to the search committee (or board if the board chooses to make this choice) a couple of firms to make presentations. Normally, a search firm will give the board a day with no fee attached, only expenses. One valuable exercise search firms ordinarily provide is to lead the board through the process of articulating the desired characteristics of the next president.

Campus decision makers will learn much about the search process by listening to these potential search firm representatives. Good questions should be developed in advance, reflecting the major areas of concern about the search. Here are just a few:

1. How many searches for presidents at campuses similar to ours have you completed?

2. How many searches do you conduct at the same time?

3. Could you describe your typical search process?

4. About how long should our search take?

5. What are your fees and when are they paid?

A Hybrid Approach

For three to five days of consulting fees and maybe two or three trips to campus, some experienced consultants will advise a search committee but not conduct the actual search for candidates nor do the reference checks on them. Also, some consultants will do the back-office role only. Some of the tasks for such a consultant might include the following:

1. Orient the search committee about the steps in the process.

2. Help devise a reasonable schedule and budget.

3. Advise the committee on the campus needs assessment.

4. Draft some of the tracking forms and letters to sources, candidates, references, and so forth.

5. Train the volunteers in good telephone and live interviewing skills.

For perhaps one-third the cost of a retained search firm, this approach will reduce the mistakes that volunteers can easily make and give additional credibility to the search process. But the board must be willing to put in hundreds of hours of volunteer time for this approach to work smoothly.

Summary

The go or no-go decision on a search firm is critical to a successful transition. Start with the assumption that you will use one, forcing the alternative approaches to prove more valuable. Choose a firm wisely and give its consultants the best cooperation possible.

Chapter 15
Role of the Incumbent President

Because of the varying situations surrounding a president's departure, there are few generalizations about how to work with the outgoing president in the search process. But incumbent presidents are a more useful resource than most search committees admit.

Let's start with the outgoing president who is not leaving under a cloud and continues to have the best interests of the campus at heart. The main direction from the board should be to urge that the outgoing president contribute to the short and long-term well-being of a campus. Although most agree that a president takes on the liabilities of a lame duck the moment a departure is announced, interested presidents and board chairs can make it clear that the board expects the president to stay focused on an agreed-upon set of goals. Good examples include completion of a capital campaign or building project.

Some outgoing presidents believe, as a matter of principle, that they should stay out of the search in every respect. They may be disciplined enough not even to discuss the search informally with friends. While one might try to dissuade them of the value of this position, it must be honored.

Those more open to helping should not force their involvement. But if a good relationship with the board continues, here are some of the ways an outgoing president can be helpful to a successful search:

1. Suggest the critical needs of the college in the next five to ten years.

2. Suggest criteria that contribute to success at the institution.

3. Suggest colleagues throughout the country who would be good sources for names of potential candidates.

4. Be available to talk about the campus to finalists, by phone or in person.

5. Host the top candidate, including a visit to the campus-owned president's house, for the prospective new occupants.

6. Make plans to introduce the new president to the campus in ways that show mutual respect and signify a positive transition.

Search committees should not expect an outgoing president to find candidates, interview them as part of the screening process, or check their references, although a handful of incumbent presidents have done some of these things with considerable success. After all, it is a maxim of searches that the best candidates need to be convinced to consider the job. And who better to convince them than a happy incumbent who has announced his intention to leave? Candidates need honest answers to their questions.

Again, do not discount a major asset, the incumbent, when planning a search. But there must be good understandings about the boundaries of this role and constant monitoring by the search committee chair.

Chapter 16
Campus Vision and Stage of Development

Announcements for new presidents often outline every characteristic of the best presidents who ever existed. But no single person ever manifests more than a few of these highly desired attributes.

A critical phase of a good presidential search is the institutional assessment. Done properly, it could make the difference between success and mere survival for the new appointee. Charles Neff and Barbara Leondar point out the sad state of affairs: "The practice of deriving presidential criteria from an appraisal of an institution's present condition and future prospects is conventional wisdom in theory and largely ignored in practice." (Neff, 1992)

There are many ways of assessing the stage of development as well as the major strengths, weaknesses, opportunities, and challenges of a particular institution. (The well-known SWOT analysis—strengths, weaknesses, opportunities, and threats—is a simple but often powerful exercise in which several campus constituencies could be involved.) Neff also quotes Judith McLaughlin and David Riesman on this topic. Every board should read this twice before forging ahead with a search:

> *"If a successful search is to be conducted, the search committee must have a clear sense of the sort of person for whom they are searching. The starting point of the search process, then, should be introspection concerning what the institution needs in order to recognize strengths and to cope with weaknesses, both in terms of history and tradition, and future prospects and dilemmas. Without an institutional assessment and leadership definition, the search committee is also at a loss to know who will be the best choice for them. They run the risk of choosing someone totally inappropriate for their institution, someone whose attractiveness lies in the fact that his or her style differs from the departing president, or someone whose understanding of the college or university is too limited for effective leadership." (Neff, 1992)*

Former AGB vice president and former executive search executive Nancy Axelrod devotes a section of her book on succession planning to this matter of institutional assessment. Although not focused exclusively on college presidents, *Succession Planning: The Board's Role in Securing Your Organization's Future* is worth reading. She writes: "The objective here is to illuminate the salient institutional issues the next chief executive is expected to take on." (Axelrod, 2002) Axelrod comments on eight areas for assessment: mission, vision, financing, governance, management, communications, institutional culture, and general questions. She mentions that good published assessment tools are available from the Amherst Wilder Foundation and the Drucker Foundation.

Without that understanding, a search committee may be taken in by a charismatic leader who makes a good first impression but whose natural gifts are not commensurate with the institution's needs.

In addition to good institutional assessments, it is imperative that the search committee conduct thorough assessments of the final candidates to be sure of that critical "good fit." Most of us cannot intuitively make those connections, so we rely on resumes and reference checks. Two good books worth exploring to fully understand the importance of and ways to discover individual gifts are *The Power of Uniqueness* (Miller) and *Now, Discover Your Strengths* (Buckingham, Clifton).

A successful presidency is almost always preceded by a good institutional assessment to identify the major needs a new president must address well, translating that consensus into the list of leadership criteria, and selecting some means to ensure that final candidates have what it takes to make the successful match.

Chapter 17
The Search Itself

There are a hundred little steps in conducting a presidential search that add up to an excellent search—or a mediocre one. No two searches are alike. The personalities involved are one inevitable variant. A board chair from the corporate sector might want to conduct the search the way it is done in his marketplace. Someone from the academy or other professions might be more sensitive to the importance of inclusion, process, and transparency. If you use a search firm, each one has practices that work best for it.

Private colleges are not subject to the open-meeting laws found in most states, so confidentiality is not an issue. More important is the campus culture. For example, a denominationally owned campus might conduct an informal search using leaders from the denomination. A campus with strong faculty leaders might demand more interaction with the candidates. Candidates would do well to understand how various campus constituencies interacted in the last search.

Timing, of course, often drives boards to do things they might not otherwise do. Many searches conclude in February or March, giving the new president time to tie up loose ends and prepare to take over at the end of the academic year. Consequently, some late-starting searches rush some important steps. In such instances, an interim president might be a better choice, giving the board time to do a proper search (see Chapter 4).

The Resources section contains several titles on the subject of presidential search that are worth reading.

Chapter 18
Being a Finalist

You've waited for weeks and weeks. Maybe no word. Then, "I'm calling to congratulate you on being one of our three finalists." Your life changes overnight. Obviously, you have thought about the exchanges of e-mails and the request for more references. You have worked hard on your essay to the search committee. But you also were busy with your day job.

Now you must take this possibility seriously. Your mind races. Do I really want this job? How long do I have? Who should I tell that I am a finalist? The questions are endless.

First, if you are one of the approximately 20 percent of presidents who take a second presidency, now is the time to confide in your board chair that you are a serious candidate and to tell the search committee that it's now okay to call your board chair. But insist on confidentiality until you learn that you are the leading candidate. Sure, there is risk involved. You may change your mind, or they might. But have this confidence: If the new job is the right one, the risk is worth it, and you want the search committee to be absolutely confident you are the best fit. If you are not sure, you don't want the job.

Gathering Information About the New Possibility

You should have good help from the search committee in gathering additional information to help you prepare for the upcoming interviews. Don't be shy. The American Council on Education published "The Well-Informed Candidate" (Atwell, 2001) just for you. This 18-page booklet suggests what information to ask for and good questions to ask of the search committee. It discusses issues in 12 categories: institutional mission and strategy; campus culture and climate; the question of fit; finances; enrollment and financial aid; faculty, staff, and curriculum; student life; information technology; governance; athletics; alumni and separate foundations; and community relations.

While it may be daunting to collect so much information, good research at this stage prevents some of the surprises that typically derail many new presidents.

Involving Your Confidants

Many presidents think it is valuable to articulate their interest and then respond to questions from family members and friends who know them best. To be pursued for a college or university presidency is heady stuff. It is not the time to be strong-willed or too casual. If the potential job seems a good fit for you, let those who love and care for you affirm that hunch. Your confidants also might be helpful in contacting people who work at the institution that interests you for information.

Visiting the Campus

If possible, make an unannounced visit to the town and campus. Most people will not know you, and some might be willing to share their thoughts about the community and campus life. Drive by the president's home. Get a feel for the community. Do you feel drawn to it, more excited the more you see? Along with the research from afar, checking your feelings for the place is helpful.

As an Internal Candidate

Since nearly one-quarter of new college presidents of private institutions already were employed by their institution, you may be one of those. You already know a lot about the school! Perhaps talking with colleagues at other institutions, state association executives, even a few trustees (with permission of your president and search committee chair) would be useful. You can't appear too eager, but you must help the search committee appreciate that you are thinking in ways you never needed to before learning that you were a finalist.

Internal candidates generally face a difficult path. Maybe the hurdle is a little higher because you are so well known. Remember, most search committees think there is an "ideal person" out there who can ride into town on a white horse and solve all the problems in one year.

The Formal Campus Visit

Be prepared and be yourself. Your spouse typically will be invited to be part of the interviews. Be sure you know the agenda, and dress appropriately for each occasion. Know who will be in the several group interviews and what the search executive or search committee chair thinks you should be prepared to discuss.

Remember that strong candidates often impress the search committee more by the thoughtful and insightful questions they ask as by the brilliant answers they give. If you made it this far, you are good! Try not to conjure up some version of an ideal candidate and pretend you are someone you're not. Let the character and personality that got you this far carry you through the interviews.

The Wait

It may take weeks for the search committee to interview other candidates. The wait can be excruciating. Take the time to review your information, and make a list of the things you will want in any employment agreement (see Chapter 19). Be sure your spouse and family are with you. Pay attention to their feelings and anxieties. You can see what could be ahead for you, but they are less certain.

Anticipate how you will respond should you not be the final choice. Who would you tell right away? How would you thank the search committee for their consideration? How would you convince your colleagues who were aware of your candidacy that you are ready to refocus on your current job? Either way, leaving or staying, having gone this far requires some mental and emotional adjustments. If someone else got the job, you did not lose. Accept the experience as important to your growth, and be thankful you did not move to a job that was not the best for you.

Chapter 19
Compensation and Benefits Package

There is only one time in the life of a presidency to get a comprehensive, fair employment package, and it is right before you say, "I'll take the job." Boards hire and fire presidents, but many have not given adequate consideration to conditions of employment beyond the salary figure. Final candidates often are so thrilled to be tapped that they overlook the compensation and benefits, not wanting to appear greedy.

Boards and candidates need to think twice. It is important to both parties that this phase of the transition is done well. It is neither a simple nor a quick task. Ideally, someone on the board has been anticipating this phase of the search and has gathered information about the institution's benefits package—perhaps comparative compensation data gathered by national or state associations—and given thought to any unique family needs that should be recognized in a final employment agreement.

A high salary alone hardly makes the job worth it. If you have received an offer, this is the time to consider what factors will help you maintain a positive attitude, what are your family's needs, and what is legal within the changing IRS regulations. Some benefits may not have dollar figures tied to them, but specific understandings that will eliminate confusion later on. You should be doing some of your own research in anticipation of negotiating a time or two on a written employment agreement.

Because you and your spouse will think of things once you are in the job for a few months, your written terms of employment should anticipate a formal revisiting of the document at some specific point in time.

Some private college presidents have multiple-year contracts, although it is not necessarily a good idea to ask for one. Consider it carefully if that has been the practice of the institution. The important thing is to get it all in writing.

Here's a laundry list of topics that might be considered in putting together an employment agreement:

1. Salary (review recent surveys for college presidents)

2. Formal fringe benefits available to all administrators, including pension benefits

3. Term of employment (either open-ended or fixed, subject to formal extension)

4. Vacation

5. Provision for performance evaluations

6. Housing or housing allowance (including house and grounds maintenance)

7. Agreement on any needed redecoration of the president's home

8. Automobile or car allowance

9. Entertainment and memberships

10. Faculty tenure

11. Sabbaticals

12. Deferred compensation

13. Special insurance

14. Travel expectations or limitations

15. Treatment of honoraria, royalties

16. Opportunity to consult with other organizations

17. Spousal salary or honoraria for campus-related duties

18. Home entertainment expenses for campus-related events

19. President's discretionary fund for new programs

20. Bridge loan if needed for the move to campus

21. Costs of selling a house and moving expenses

22. Tuition waiver or subsidy for children

23. Delegation of responsibilities in case of severe illness

24. Post-presidential responsibilities or opportunities

25. Severance pay if involuntarily terminated

26. Other matters important to the president or the institution

Once a board and candidate have come to an oral agreement, everyone is relieved and elated. But the hard work of a fair and comprehensive employment agreement should not be short-changed. Both sides will benefit if all possibilities are considered up front. Then the work can begin.

Chapter 20
Public Announcement

The work of a search is almost done. Now to let those on campus, people at the successful candidate's home base, and the general public hear the good news. Again, this seemingly simple step has the potential to advance or set back any campus. The board chair or the chair of the search committee should coordinate with the newly selected president, the campus communications director, and others to see that each task is handled well.

The following constituents, in roughly this order, should be told the news:

1.   The chosen candidate's current employer

2.   Board members who were not present for the final vote

3.   Members of the search committee who are not on the board

4.   The campus communications officer

5.   The entire campus

6.   Unsuccessful candidates (ideally, letters to all nominees)

7.   Alumni and donors

8.   Presidents of peer institutions and national associations

9.   The general public

This all takes time and should contribute to the public relations of the campus. The entire campus needs to hear the news within a day of others being told, an announcement that should come from the board chair. This could be an e-mail to everyone on the campus system and could contain basic information about the new president plus an invitation to a campus convocation.

Such a convocation can be informal or an event that calls forth all the regalia of a commencement. The objectives are to thank the search committee, give a report of their good work, acknowledge the contributions of the incumbent, and introduce the president-designee (and family if possible). Ideally, the president and his successor should publicly pledge to each other their cooperation for an outstanding transition.

Sadly, the planned communications suggested above often leave out the finalists in the search or the successful candidate's employer and colleagues. Notices to all nominees, along with a genuine expression of thanks for their interest, can all be accomplished within the same hour as a public notice if it is planned in advance. That adds to the good name of the university.

On the day after the public announcement, a copy of the media release should be sent to each of the nominees, those who nominated them, key alumni, and major donors. Naturally, this requires that someone has been asked to anticipate this task and is prepared to do it in a timely fashion.

The announcements also can summarize the work of the search committee, the timetable for the transition, and perhaps the plans of the incumbent. These letters, phone calls, media interviews, and mass e-mails give another lasting impression of your institution. Yes, this next-to-last step in a search is worth doing well.

Chapter 21
Wrapping Up

The last formal step often is neglected in the euphoria of selecting a new president. Someone has to organize and secure the committee's files, ensure that all travel reimbursements have been completed, and other important tasks that can improve the next search.

Let's hope the campus will not have to do another search for ten years. Whenever the date, however, a few hours of wrap-up work by the search committee chair and search secretary can save endless hours and several missteps the next time around. Everyone has learned something that could be improved the next time around.

Here is a short list of things that should be considered before the search wraps up:

1. Send letters and small gifts to the search committee members.

2. Send letters to all who helped with the search.

3. Conduct a debriefing with the search firm, if one was used.

4. Conduct a debriefing with finalists to learn what the campus could do better the next time from their perspective. Some even give the finalists candid feedback on their strengths and weaknesses to assist them in their career planning.

5. Discuss how the incumbent was or was not used in the search to anticipate the best practice for the next time around.

6. Pay all bills and prepare a financial summary for the file.

7. Ask search committee members for memos on their experiences to guide future searches.

These tasks should stimulate other useful ideas. The search committee chair should assume responsibility for most of this wrap-up stage. As in all of education, evaluation is an important part of learning.

Preparing for a New Presidency

Chapter 22
Finishing the Current Job Well

This section applies most to presidents who are moving to a new presidency.

Reflecting on his experience when leaving an 18-year presidency of a private college, Richard Richter said, "A conscious effort to preserve the institution's pace and a clear and substantial agenda for the president's final months can make the difference between ending a presidency with the satisfaction of a job well done or ineffectually fading away." (Richter, 1995)

If, indeed, any president is accorded lame-duck status and the limited attention and authority that go with it, it is important for the board and the outgoing president to consider the matter of timing and a plan for the period of remaining service.

A key matter to consider when completing a presidency is the status of vital projects. Such a list might include completion of a fund-raising campaign, implementation of a strategic plan, dedication of a major campus building, or completion of an accreditation review. Successful resolution of these can position the institution well for a successor and bring deserved accolades for the departing president. The timing in announcing such successes during the year should allow for celebration of the leadership of the outgoing president and provide opportunities to introduce the newly elected president.

Finishing the job well also means that the departing president should do everything possible to maintain a strong support staff for the incoming president, ensure a balanced budget for the current fiscal year, establish a sound budget for the first year of the next presidency, enhance good town-gown relationships, and provide praise for the successor. The departing president should also refrain from "cleaning house" but rather give his or her successor a complete view as to whom to fire or retain. Introductions to key "difference makers" at the institution are also a nice touch.

Finding ways to sustain well-earned momentum should be a major goal during a president's last year. One key action is to write or call major supporters of the institution to encourage them to continue their interest and dedication by assisting the incoming chief executive. This personal touch is also a nice way to express thanks for past support.

A successful presidency often concludes with many significant gestures of praise. Often, a president may be in the position of steering a major gift in his honor to meet an area of real need for the institution. When this is done, there is a feeling of satisfaction that not only serves as a reward but shortens the list of things that must be done by a successor. Leaving a place better than you found it is a grand feeling that remains for many years. Making sure that things are in place for the institution to continue to thrive is the last great gesture you can make in saying farewell.

Chapter 23
Learning More About the New Campus

No matter how much homework presidential candidates complete, the incoming president soon becomes aware that there is so much to learn and so little time. The task now depends on how well the search committee has prepared the finalists—and how well the incoming president has prepared for the job. Learning about the history and culture of the institution is absolutely critical to a good launch, and the time between the board's announcement of a new president and the president's first day of work is a great time to focus on this.

People change slowly and with some difficulty. Each campus community has an ethos that can give an outsider the feeling of being, well, an outsider. So how does the incoming president penetrate that culture?

It may be helpful for the board or the incumbent president to appoint a campus transition committee. This small group of campus leaders could gather relevant materials, including histories of the campus, annual reports, audits, alumni magazines, key presidential statements of recent years, accreditation visit reports, news reports, and planning documents.

Other actions a new president might take to speed the learning curve include independent conversations with the board chair, past board chairs, past presidents and spouses, presidents of neighboring institutions, retired senior officers, national and regional higher education association heads, local governmental representatives, accreditation body heads, church leaders, and the institution's auditor. Information obtained from such contacts can substantiate early impressions and validate information provided by the institution. Personal revelations help identify anticipated areas of concern and how deeply those most affected by them feel about their resolution. It will help determine which priorities require immediate attention and which can wait for a longer period.

The ability to avoid early pitfalls and mistakes generally depends on how well an incoming president can read the culture of the institution. An informed perspective comes from excellent preparation. A genuine interest in learning more about the community will pay dividends in creating a good first impression. It shows you have a real interest in understanding the culture of the workplace and community that sustains it.

Apart from learning about the campus per se, many newly appointed presidents find it helpful to attend one of several new presidents' orientation or training programs sponsored by a university or national association. Some of these include spouses, board chairs, and other cabinet officers. A new president might even ask a friend who has been in a similar presidency to convene a handful of presidents for a long weekend to discuss current challenges. Any new president will benefit from having colleagues who are willing to be called when another president is the only one who can answer a newcomer's question.

Chapter 24
Family and Housing Issues

Everything is a whirl for a family preparing to leave one community and become a college's first family in another. Depending on the schedule and circumstances, this can be very stressful. Each situation is unique, so it is difficult to provide a list of best practices. The purpose of this chapter is to remind the board, which just completed its search, that important leadership tasks remain for them to oversee.

The new president's family is just beginning their hard work. There may be a home to sell; perhaps a spouse may need to leave a job and seek another; there may be school, church, and health-care changes; children's emotions must be taken into account—there are so many unknowns.

One of the best things a board can do is establish a family transition committee. Candidates for this group might include a trustee or two, spouses of trustees who live in the immediate area, a cabinet officer, faculty or faculty spouses, and someone from the business office. The group's mandate is to stay in touch with the family on all needs not directly related to the president's job and to facilitate information gathering, local contacts, interim housing options if necessary, and related tasks.

One aspect of many new moves is to assess the state of the campus-owned president's house. It is natural for the house to need some new paint, wallpaper, and perhaps appliances. A task force or subgroup of the transition committee should be given a budget by the board and instructed to work with the incoming president's family to determine what should be done and when. A newly arrived family risks criticism for spending money on itself the first few months on campus, but a campus that anticipates and facilities a "fresh new home" for the family gets high marks.

It is common in private colleges for spouses to be offered campus jobs if their qualifications fit specific needs. (See Chapter 19 for spousal compensation other than campus employment.) This, too, can be a sensitive area for a president to have to take the lead. While this might be discussed in the last stages of the search and employment agreements, it could be something for the board chair to initiate once the family is settled.

Presidents and their spouses are expected to assume various responsibilities regarding hospitality, so campus officials should anticipate such matters as the availability of campus help, arrangements for expenses, and so forth.

If the family has children, the family will need help meeting peers, deciding where to attend school, and learning about recreational opportunities. Such niceties distinguish a helpful from an unhelpful transition committee.

Chapter 25
Board Relations Prior to Start Date

The board chair (or search committee chair, but it needs to be clear) normally takes the initiative to stay in touch with the newly chosen president. This key element of transition is weakened if the board has decided to change chairs at the same time the new president arrives—not an uncommon event.

There are myriad issues, some small to be sure, that come up during the preparation phase, but newly selected presidents may find it awkward "bothering" the board chair every time a question comes up.

Beyond a designated "go to" trustee, and the family transition committee, some boards appreciate periodic reports from the incoming president. Again, sensitivity to the incumbent and clarification of expectations is important. The chair may want to recommend to the board and incumbent that a simple monthly memo to the board is appropriate.

Some boards meet only two or three times a year. The normal cycle of board business related to budgets, planning, fund-raising, and so forth must go on. So it is appropriate that the incoming president be briefed on board business and invited to comment on issues being prepared for the next board meeting. Normally, the incoming president would not attend a board meeting prior to assuming office—but it would not be unusual if everyone thought that to be a good idea.

The preparation time might include an overlap of employment with the incumbent. This happens naturally if an internal candidate has been selected. Guided by circumstances, a few weeks or even a couple months could be a wise investment on the board's part.

Certain habits of the board will guide these issues. On the other hand, if a new chair is elected to coincide with the arrival of a new president, this is a good time to reevaluate customs and initiate some common sense and creative practices. The board's committee on trusteeship may have pertinent suggestions to guide this set of decisions. While waiting for a new president to arrive, some boards may find it worthwhile to conduct a self-assessment (see Chapter 38).

Chapter 26
Campus Visits Prior to Start Date

The incumbent president and the board should lead on the question of whether, why, when, and how an incoming president visits the campus. A few visits are a good idea. Similarly, ongoing calls or e-mails normally should be guided by the incumbent. An incoming president who comes across as too eager risks getting off on the wrong foot.

What is best for the campus? When a successful president is happily retiring or moving on to another position with the best wishes of a campus, there is often great benefit to the campus to observe the two leaders working closely together. Two who modeled this well were the outgoing and incoming presidents of Wilson College. (Edmundson, 2003) They worked closely on what incoming president Lorna Duphiney Edmundson needed to get off to a strong start.

From their experience, and from others' suggestions, here is a good list to consider for the time between the public announcement and the official start date:

- Agree on things to read.

- Schedule weekly phone calls.

- Invite the incoming president to serve as an in-house consultant.

- Invite the outgoing president to serve as a mentor.

- Introduce the new president to the local media, business leaders, and major donors.

- Facilitate the new president's appointment to important boards in the area.

- Copy the incoming president on campus e-mail lists.

- Work together on an important job search and agree on the choice.

- Hold a campus convocation to pass the baton.

- Visit a faculty meeting, retreat, or cabinet meeting.

- Attend commencement.

- Receive important administrative reports.

The details are less important than the spirit of collaboration. In the case of Wilson College, this partnership continued after the new president assumed office. The retired president was invited back to celebrate the completion of a successful capital campaign for which she was primarily responsible and to travel on an alumni trip to Italy. Unusual? Perhaps. Other incoming and outgoing presidents who worked closely offer additional lessons:

- Do everything with the understanding and encouragement of the board.

- Keep the activities mission driven, not personality driven.

- Balance honoring the past with anticipating the future.

- Be clear to staff and others that the incumbent is still the chief executive.

- Allow either person to politely opt out of an idea the other suggests.

- Honor the need of the outgoing president to finish well and attend to family needs.

When the departing president is unable or unwilling to provide this kind of helpful transition assistance, the incoming president can be in a bind. Again, the board chair may be able to help coordinate some plans and appoint one of the vice presidents to assume the lead on facilitating campus visits, briefings, appointments, and the like.

It certainly is true that good transitions do occur with very little communication and joint appearances during the changing of the guard. Yet a sensitive approach to presidential transition is of greater benefit than is normally assumed.

Launching a New Presidency

Chapter 27
Arrival and the First 90, 180, 365 Days

The day arrives! If you show up on July 1, the campus may look dead, with many people on vacation. You walk across campus, and hardly anyone will recognize you. At the grocery store, they've never heard of you.

Or...everyone in your cabinet is in the office when you walk in. Volunteers are at your new home when the van arrives. People bring in food for the family's first night. Your parents are secretly invited to a welcome party the following Saturday. It makes a difference which of these scenarios greets you on day one.

Today you are the new chief executive. Your new boss is called the board of trustees—and don't ever forget it! You have new staff you did not select but all are wondering just how they should relate to you. People in food service, physical plant, the book store, and the athletic department (well, maybe) are all anxious to please you if only they could figure out how. Mail has been saved. Appointments have been made for you.

You feel overwhelmed. That's okay. But now you must show whether you are in control of your work or are captive of it. Remember you are the institution to many constituencies. Many new presidents say their best move was to have a plan of action in mind when they arrived. A useful rule of thumb is to use one-half of your time to be proactive on your thought-through agenda. The rest of the hours "just happen" as part of this unrelenting 24/7 job.

Think about putting together a 90-180-365 day plan that will give you a view of the complete annual cycle. A campus calendar already exists that you will integrate into your own plan. Other questions to consider in putting your plan together include the following:

- Who must be seen one-on-one in the first days?

- Which groups should you convene early on?

- Which groups are you automatically part of, and when do they meet?

- Should you set up both a personal and a president's e-mail address?

- Are there vacancies you must fill or create?

- When do you say that you will lay out your ideas to implement your own vision? (Most suggest after at least 180 days in the job.)

- How do you want your staff to organize your work flow?

- And many more...

Those who have tracked presidents' first years have some interesting conclusions. Judith Block McLaughlin, who chaired the Harvard Seminar for New Presidents, writes, "A carefully planned and executed entry becomes the new president's first act of leadership." She continues, "My research suggests that new presidents are at greater risk of moving too rapidly than of proceeding too cautiously." (McLaughlin, 1996)

Naturally, parts of any first-year plan need consultation with the board to ensure that it shares your priorities. Certainly, the board chair must be kept informed, and your vice presidents need to feel their input is important. Much of your plan will be adjusted when the realities of the office force modifications.

After several weeks, people's first impressions give way to judgments about you based on results. What the community is not "up on," they will probably be "down on." So you need to communicate especially well.

The principle in this chapter is simply to be prepared with a game plan. Then be flexible. New presidents should not try too hard to impose their own plan and style without recognizing that many others feel that they "own" part of the president's time. There are many protocols and customs to be learned and honored, and listening and learning are keys to refining the plan on a regular basis.

Chapter 28
Relationships with Campus Leaders

There await on campus key individuals and groups who have put many things on hold, including their own emotions and career plans. If you have used the time leading up to your arrival to involve these folks in appropriate ways, the need now is reduced. But some boards or departing presidents do not encourage these efforts. In too many situations, the first time that the president has held conversations with cabinet officers, faculty senate leaders, and others whose roles are closely linked to the president's leadership is the new leader's first week on the job.

Your own leadership style, the degree to which you have had help from a transition committee, the time of year you arrive, and the state of the campus all affect how you relate to these key campus leaders. Do you ask for letters of resignation from those reporting to you, with the understanding that you may not act on them but reserve the right to do so within a year? Or do you say, "I will make no changes in those reporting to me for at least one year until I get to know you all well?" Both approaches can work. Nevertheless, these people often fear the worst, assuming their jobs are on the line. You should be sensitive to this natural anxiety.

How do you manage? Everyone is looking for clues to this question. Ask for input from those who reported to you in the past, so you have a good read on how others perceive you. Maybe you want to start off doing some things differently in this position. When you call the first cabinet meeting, for example, is it an informal get-together in your home, or is it in the conference room with a formal agenda? How do you describe the function of cabinet meetings? Is it a decision-making group in which each individual has a vote, a consensus-building group in which you determine when consensus is achieved, a meeting for you to gather feedback for your own decisions, or simply a sharing time in which each individual brings items the others need to know? Or is it all of the above? Be clear.

A good rule to remember is that "most miscommunication is a result of differing assumptions." For a new president, the assumption is that people do what they did with the former president until told differently. New presidents can launch their presidencies assuming they will do things the way they did them before—just remember that no one else knows those things until you explain them! Having a good right-hand administrator, often the chief academic officer, who has the trust of people on campus is extraordinarily important to you in helping interpret your desires to the community.

Everyone feels honored when asked for an opinion or invited to brief a new president on some topic. Use these times for active listening. Be a student of other people's work. Because faculty support is essential to your success, be slow to prescribe exactly how you will relate to the faculty senate, faculty committees, and so forth. What has worked well in the past for them? What suggestions do they have for the president's role in academic affairs? Remember that even when the board says that you are the chief academic officer, many others on campus believe differently, including the individual who has that title! Only in academia, right?!

Students are watching your every move. Will you be friend or foe to their interests? While student interest in world affairs seems to be growing after years of relative disinterest, do you want to relate to students on small internal matters or challenge them to engage you on broader ethical, political, or humanitarian issues? Students and others on campus are wondering such basic things as, "Do we call him Dr. Newman, or Dr. Sam, or just Sam? How about Sam's wife? What do we call her? These and dozens of more profound questions are waiting for clarity, and you have the chance to shape the answers.

An important relationship issue is the matter of delegation. While you may be motivated to show an interest in everything and to respond to all who bring decisions to your desk, the first few months is a good time for you to learn to delegate more than you might be accustomed. It could save your presidency. No president can do everything others expect, so this is the time to teach them that when you delegate a task, you will not interfere. Allow your cabinet officers to share in personnel decisions and strategies. This is one reason a strong staff is critical.

Finally, seeking wisdom from other presidents before you arrive and maintaining peer relationships with colleagues who can be confidants in your early days are essential elements for success. Whether on campus or in your external duties, maintaining good relationships will be a preoccupation.

Chapter 29
Honoring and Involving Your Predecessor

Beyond saying the principle is to honor and involve your predecessor in appropriate ways, there are few "must do's" here.

If you inherited a board-brokered employment agreement between the board and your predecessor, you will need to sort out with the board how that will work from your perspective. There may be a written document to guide the conversation. If you discover something intolerable in that agreement, now is the time to address it with the board chair. If you can live with it, there are still mutual understandings that must be worked out to complement rather than conflict with your leadership. It's important to craft a memorandum of understanding to capture for the record what you and your predecessor have agreed to do.

Here are some suggestions that might prove helpful:

1. Put your predecessor on any e-mail, fax, or mailing lists.

2. Ask your predecessor and spouse whether there are any unresolved issues regarding their move from campus. This might include reimbursements of expenses, retrieval of items mistakenly left in the president's house, needed copies of documents, and so forth. You never know.

3. Use your first column in the alumni magazine to acknowledge your predecessor's record of achievement and post-presidency plans.

4. Look ahead at the list of campus events and decide whether and how you might include your predecessor at convocations, donor dinners, and alumni events.

5. Consider whether a scholarship or fellowship, a capital project, or some other project might both honor your predecessor and allow loyal donors to do something that makes everyone feel good.

6. Call your predecessor if you have to make a major decision that might be embarrassing or unwelcome news. This is not only courteous, but it could prevent adverse media coverage or a divided campus.

The principle is simple: Honor your predecessor and you help yourself, the campus, and everyone who has loyally supported the institution. Do not overlook important acts of civility. The Golden Rule applies. Someday a colleague will remind your successor of these things and you will be glad!

Chapter 30
Board Communications

While you are focusing so much on campus leaders, major donors, and influential community leaders, don't forget your employer. The board is proud of you because they selected you. They will give you a decent honeymoon period and overlook a few early missteps.

The board will also want to get back to business it may have deferred during the search. And you realize that, while your relationship with a few trustees is good, there may be others you have not met, and most of them are waiting to see how you communicate with the board once you are on the job.

These key volunteers do not think about the campus every day. And when they do, their attention is usually guided by you. The average 30 private college trustees, especially if they have no term limits, may include some who have seen many presidents come and go. Learn from these veteran trustees. And learn how the chair, the "manager of the board," likes to communicate with you, the "chief executive of the campus." This president-board chair relationship is more important to your job effectiveness than any other relationship except the one with your spouse.

Here are some guidelines for good communication with the board chair:

1. Suggest weekly phone calls with the chair so you're on the same page. All trustees should know that these phone calls occur.

2. Visit each trustee in his or her home. Meet the spouse, seek ideas on how to improve the board, learn what motivates each to serve, and listen for ways to involve each trustee and spouse in volunteer activities that fit special interests. Take your spouse on these first visits if possible.

3. Send monthly one-page memoranda to the board with updates on campus events, your key activities, and something on the family. Some presidents do this with e-mails or faxes. Be sure not to leave anyone out who does not have the requisite technology.

4. Four weeks before the first board meeting, schedule conference calls with the board chair, each committee chair, and the executive who staffs each board committee. Brief the trustees on what you would like to see on the committee's agenda, ask for input from the committee chair, and invite suggestions for improving the committee meetings.

5. Two weeks before the first board meeting, send an excellent board book with a few enhancements to what the board is used to seeing. Include a good president's report as well as short written reports from the vice presidents. Add something new and helpful, perhaps a new tracking or monitoring system on board priorities.

6. Work with your assistant on a system to acknowledge board member birthdays and/or anniversaries. Send a short note with an article or report when you know that a trustee has a particular interest.

7. Look for special meetings sponsored by state or national associations that might be good to share with your board chair or executive committee members.

Chapter 31
The Inauguration

Not all new presidents want a formal inauguration. Like some facing a wedding, they would prefer to elope and forgo the hassles and costs. A new president, consulting with board and faculty leaders, should assess the history of the campus, when the last inauguration was held and how it went, and evaluate the pros and cons of doing one now. Inaugurations are not required by law, but they have a long and distinguished tradition in the academy. They come in all shapes and sizes.

While the president should have the largest voice in the decision, an inauguration is a community event, and others should be consulted before a conclusion is reached one way or the other. If the consensus is not to have a full-blown event with outside guests, some campuses will opt for a more modest celebration or ceremony as part of another event such as commencement or homecoming.

What follows are some highlights from *Presidential Inaugurations: Planning for More than Pomp and Circumstance*, published by the Council for Advancement and Support of Education. Based on a survey of more than 100 campuses in the early 1990s, this is perhaps the best "how to" book available. Here are ten key concerns the book raises for those charged with running a presidential inauguration:

1. Does the president want a full-blown inauguration consisting of several events or simply a presidential installation ceremony?

2. For a full inauguration, count on at least six months of planning and pick a date within the first year of office.

3. Choose an administrator who knows the campus well, pays attention to details, and can delegate effectively as chair of an inaugural committee.

4. Develop a theme and guiding principles, specific goals and objectives, along with physical and fiscal parameters.

5. Appoint many subcommittees for specific tasks; involve the campus and the community in planning.

6. Reserve all the facilities that might be needed.

7. Coordinate the many printed materials that must be done well in advance.

8. Agree on total costs. In the survey for this book, 80 percent of campuses staged their inaugurations for less than $50,000 (remember that was in 1990-92 dollars). Determine which budgets will be tapped and which donors might be asked to help.

9. Decide which of the thousands of possible invitees will actually be invited and to which events. Are addresses easily obtainable? Who will gather that information? How will RSVPs be handled? Who should be the VIP invitees, and how will they be involved in the programs?

10. Decide what will be done and by whom during the installation ceremony. If the event is to be held outdoors, develop a weather-related contingency plan.

Clearly, having a few people on campus who helped organize a previous inauguration is a big help. Inviting an inauguration committee chair from a sister campus to share materials and brief the cabinet would be a great help.

As a new president, you should be aware that many people will misread or disagree with the preferences you state for your inauguration. Some will question not doing a full celebration because of the public-relations benefits to the campus. But others will question the costs if the campus is struggling with its operating budgets. Consider whether the campus needs the "boost" of pulling off a major event successfully that requires everyone to work together. Personal humility and campus pride are difficult virtues to merge on this topic.

As with all major decisions, a new president should consult with the board chair. Ultimately, how the board responds to the final decisions and the events themselves is very important to a successful first year.

Whatever you decide about a full-blown inauguration or a more simple installation ceremony, know that your leadership style and your aspirations for the campus can be displayed in powerful ways. The inauguration has the potential to be one of the best opportunities of your presidency to both lead and share the spotlight with others, to engage community, political, church, and business leaders in the life of the campus, and to improve the self-esteem of the entire campus and community.

Chapter 32
Handling the Big Surprises

What makes the presidency so exciting and challenging is the certainty that there will be unexpected events. You will be tempted to yell, "Why didn't the search committee tell me this?" The emotion is real. But it is too late to do anything but assure yourself that you can handle surprises. Not always alone. But you can handle them. Some examples:

Inaccurate financial information and statements. Accurate fiscal information about current and past budgets leads the list of things presidents most wished they had known before they accepted the job. Unfortunately, both the board and the past president may have been in the dark regarding the true budget picture. In due course, audits and budget reviews can uncover major reporting flaws. More than one new president has assumed office thinking the budget was balanced only to find that the institution had been running deficits. Poor internal controls and bad bookkeeping require swift action. If you don't understand the audit or budget accounting methods used, seek help immediately. An outside consultant and an internal audit are often essential when you find surprises. Don't put this one off.

The president's home. Not all campuses provide a president's home, and some homes are decidedly not the preference of the new presidential family. But let's assume you are destined for a college-owned home. Hours after your move in, you may discover surprises difficult for the family to handle. Updating its condition should have been agreed upon and completed before your arrival. Large or unusual expenditures at the outset of the presidency have been known to haunt presidents throughout their tenure. The price tag for renovation or purchase of a new residence has always been a matter of campus concern and can be a major source of conflict. Avoid using operating funds to handle this situation if possible. Instead, the board may wish to establish a fund to support presidential housing.

Unanticipated changes in trustee leadership. It is not unusual for a new board chair to assume the post once a new president is on the job. Key committee chairs may ask to be replaced. Some trustees, who may have backed a different candidate, might resign. These all can come as surprises. As the new president, you may have no input into the selection of the key board leaders, although good presidents later work out ways to have some say in whom they can work with best. Whether you are excited or disappointed to hear about the new board leaders, make the best of the situation and build those relationships quickly. Look to the board chair and your cabinet officers to interpret these surprises.

Sudden staff resignations. Most senior staff members remain in place until they get a read on the intentions of the new president. But some will have been looking for new jobs during the presidential search. They may announce their intent to move on during your first campus visit. Others may think it appropriate to submit a letter of resignation. Should you accept it or say you will think about it?

Some assistants to presidents develop so much loyalty that they leave when a new president is selected. Or one you have heard should be replaced decides to stay to "help you get started" even though your predecessor suggested you hire someone new. Staff surprises need careful handling because every employee has a personal history that you can't possibly know about. Ask the appropriate colleagues for background, and assure all staff that you want time to get to know them. Set mutually agreeable goals, and evaluate their performance before you make staff changes. Then start the recruitment process to fill the key positions that were vacant when you arrived.

Fund-raising surprises. In your first few months, you should not be surprised if a few major donors signal that their investments were linked to friendship with your predecessor and that their giving will be reduced. Or stopped. Maybe someone asks to change their pledge to the capital campaign because they preferred another candidate. Perhaps you will discover that a critical foundation grant needs $250,000 in matching gifts within 45 days. Ask your chief development officer to give you a heads-up about potential surprises. If appropriate, ask your predecessor to accompany you to a meeting with a major donor to help solidify the donor's relationship with the institution. Because the annual campaign and any capital campaign that is not concluded are so critical to your presidency, deal with any surprises sooner rather than later.

Simmering community issues. Town-gown relations are always highly sensitive. A new leader might be surprised at the extent of anguish over the institution's tax-exempt properties. Concern about lack of involvement with local school districts or environmental issues also tends to appear quickly. Policies on use of an institution's recreational facilities or attendance at cultural events may be lingering. In many small communities, it is not uncommon for the institution to be one of the major employers. The place of the college or university in economic development can be very significant. Improving a relationship with a mayor, city, or village board can absorb large amounts of time. Many community leaders have been waiting for the new president to arrive to spring new demands or change old understandings. Ask which people in the community need an early visit from you.

Perhaps the most unwelcome discovery will be any conflicts of interest between the institution and its local trustees. These may occur in such areas as banking, investment, real estate, and law. Tackling issues in this area will require hours of private conversations and speeches to groups. Marshall your patience, tact, and diplomacy in these areas.

Lower than expected enrollment. Nothing spoils your first year than to discover that fall enrollment will be 10 percent less than projected. Learn the reasons why fast. Are similar institutions anticipating similar shortfalls? What data were used to create the budget you inherited? How has your retention rate held up? Is there still time to gain new enrollees? Was a contingency plan developed?

Personal surprises about you. New presidents rarely know all the circumstances surrounding their selection. If there was a strong internal candidate from the faculty, staff, or trustees, then you must be sensitive to the aftermath of their not being selected. This may lead either to a resignation or a decision to stay on at the institution with the hope that their turn may come. If your selection followed the term of an acting president, particularly if it was a trustee, this may create a set of awkward dynamics that may hamper your abilities to perform your job the way you want to. Until you learn certain things directly or through confidential conversations, there is little to do other than proceed with caution. Ideally, all of the finalists for the position were outsiders, and the board and those who performed the search were unanimous in their belief that you were the right person for the job. Gradually, you will learn background information on the why and how of your appointment. Use that information wisely in forming personal relationships within the campus community.

Denomination surprises in church-related institutions. Campus politics are not the only ones some presidents face. Within 900 private religious institutions, there are church relations to understand. Campus-church relations may be on sound footing when you arrive, but there also could be active or pending issues that may take unexpected turns. Although financial support from most denominations has diminished, church relations often affect admissions policies, appointment of trustees, alumni relations, and other matters. If you do not come from within the same faith community, it might be wise to appoint a church-relations director who is familiar with the community. The challenge is to strengthen relations with the founding denomination while helping church leaders understand your need to build constituencies beyond the denomination.

All of the forgoing areas of possible surprise will give you problems you don't deserve. But you should also anticipate nice surprises, such as the unexpected gift of an endowment for faculty development or a problem faculty member who unexpectedly accepts a job at another campus. Some surprises will allow you to demonstrate why you were selected to be the chief executive.

Chapter 33
Personal and Family Priorities

By now, you may be wondering, "Is it too late to turn down this job!?" This is a good time to remind you that being president of a college is one of the most rewarding jobs in the world. You are investing in the leaders of the next generation. You are in a community of learners who keep one another informed and alert. You have a chance to model character and integrity in leadership.

To do this job well—to deal with the unrelenting pressures of your role—you must quickly find a new formula for balancing personal and family priorities with the demands of the job. You already know this. But it is important to think this through honestly and to reach understandings with your family and with those closest to you at work. No president is given a poor evaluation because he or she put too high a priority on personal health, balance in life, and on family.

You may take a morning run, have breakfast with the family, reserve an hour for reflection each day, have personal rules about Sunday work, or take a personal retreat once a year. Start with what works for you, and rely on your assistant to schedule your days. You will need to inform your cabinet of priorities that you want their help in fulfilling. Your spouse needs permission to monitor your emotional and physical pulse and say, "Stop!" when that is what you need to hear.

A chief executive does not do it all, cannot do it all, should not even try to do it all. Yet many surely behave as though it all depends on them, right? Find help. The college presidents who seem to get personal and family priorities in line do the following things well:

1. Stay physically fit. The job requires it.

2. Remember to work from your strengths and delegate areas of weakness.

3. Block out family time months in advance.

4. Invite a small group to be your confidants and support group.

5. Find a favorite nearby "get away" and go there, even for a day.

6. Set realistic expectations about what campus events you will or will not attend.

7. Have an assistant who is an effective gatekeeper.

8. Nurture your spiritual life.

9. Take the vacations to which you are entitled.

10. Do not attend the meetings you really don't need to attend.

11. Delegate things others need to do to grow.

12. Keep your priorities in writing and devote your days to achieving them.

You can add to this list. The job will be there long after you finish your turn at it. You are simply a steward for a season. But you and your family have much farther to travel.

Chapter 34
Planning Sabbaticals

An informed board should consider sabbatical leaves for presidents a necessity. This benefit, usually granted for excellent performance with the hopes a president will then stay longer, is another factor in transitions. A sabbatical can prevent burnout by giving the president time to reflect on how to recast priorities. It can even improve a marriage. There are lots of benefits and few downsides if a president has prepared the way for others to handle his or her duties during the sabbatical. In short, sabbatical leaves for presidents are justified and deserved.

Sabbaticals seldom are written into initial fixed-year contracts. If a president "serves at the pleasure" of the board, the board should take the initiative in amending any first-year agreement after five years. If it is a contractual arrangement, sabbaticals should be standard after the first one. More campuses are granting sabbaticals to administrators as well as to faculty members.

Terms for sabbaticals vary. Some presidents negotiate annual study leaves, a form of sabbatical. Others prefer a two-month or three-month sabbatical every five to seven years. And some take a semester or more after a longer tenure. Regular salary and benefits should be maintained during the sabbatical. Some institutions even provide a modest travel supplement for families. Each president should explore the pros and cons of the different arrangements.

For presidents, negotiating a sabbatical can trigger increased commitment to stay for the long haul—or it can send signals that maybe the board is not looking as far ahead as the president. It is appropriate to ask for a plan that will impart personal and professional benefits alike. Many presidents study, travel, or interview people on a subject that is critical to the future of their institutions. The timing is best evaluated a few years in advance, and its beginning often coincides with the completion of a capital campaign.

What conditions should govern the sabbatical? Should there be a written report? The best approach is to leave the purpose in the hands of the president. Travel abroad, a quiet place to write, read, or just walk a beach can do wonders for personal renewal and improved health. The idea of a mandatory, written report should not be a condition for the board granting a sabbatical, but a wise president will send periodic e-mails to the board and/or present a report on returning.

Extenuating circumstances may influence the need for a sabbatical sooner than the stipulated period designated in the contract. Some examples include changes in personal health, loss of a family member or loved one, or care for elderly parents. The periods of leaves granted under these special cases may vary greatly and usually will not follow the normal pattern.

More than one presidency has been saved by the board's insistence that the president take a leave. Sabbaticals can ensure the continued vitality of an institution by enhancing the personal self-renewal of the president and his or her family. The benefits are incalculable. The board communicates how much it values the president personally and professionally in granting sabbatical leaves.

One other form of sabbatical is common. Because many presidents are not paid what they deserve—and some insist on taking minimal leaves—some boards grant a retiring president a year's sabbatical as soon as his or her successor arrives. This gives the president and his/her family time to rediscover an identity other than the "first family," to explore options for the future, and to catch up on one's discipline, if teaching is the plan for the future. This constitutes more than deferred compensation and is often better than paying a president to stay on as a paid chancellor.

Whatever form of sabbatical a president and board decide is most meaningful, a sabbatical is a good investment for both parties. It is part of the cycle of transition for any successful presidency.

Evaluating Presidential and Board Performance

Chapter 35
Evaluating the President

The process and outcome of a presidential performance evaluation influences the tenure of every chief executive, making it another critical milestone in the cycle of presidential transitions. Several good resources are available on the topic, and only the key principles of presidential assessments are highlighted here.

Why evaluations? It is vital that the board and president understand one another and agree on priorities. Without a formal process, presidents often underestimate or overestimate how well they are performing. Some may assume the worst and decide to look elsewhere; others may be oblivious to how they are perceived. It is important for small things to be resolved so they do not become insurmountable barriers to continued service. Without exception, good evaluations are helpful to boards and presidents alike.

Timing of evaluations. Regular performance evaluations should be conducted at the end of each academic year. Normally, goals for the following year are negotiated at the same time.

Leadership of evaluations. The board is responsible for authorizing its executive committee or some other small group to lead the process. Ultimately, the chair delivers both an oral and written report to the president. An outside consultant may assist in special evaluations.

Content of evaluations. There are two basic types of evaluations. The normal approach is to agree upon reasonable performance goals and conduct an evaluation based on them. Among the topics these goals address might be finances, faculty development, fund-raising, enrollment, relationship building, media relations, academics, and board relations. Another category of evaluation, often used when people outside of the board are involved, might include more general topics such as leadership, ability to delegate responsibilities, communication skills, conflict management, character, and influence on behalf of the campus.

Annual evaluation process. There are dozens of successful models. The basics normally include a written self-evaluation by the president to the board. The executive committee then invites formal or informal feedback after seeing the self-evaluation. An executive session at the spring board meeting allows the president to answer questions. Then an executive session without the president allows trustees to discuss the chief executive's performance. The executive committee, or at least the chair on its behalf, should then give the president both an oral and written summary. At about this time, the committee and the president should agree upon the goals for the coming academic year.

Periodic comprehensive evaluations. Many campuses are moving to more elaborate evaluations conducted every three to five years. A consultant might be brought in to facilitate interviews and/or conduct surveys of key administrators, faculty members, student leaders, community officials, a few major donors, and peer presidents from similar institutions. Some use "360°" evaluations, meaning that trustees, peers, and those supervised by the president are invited to comment on the same items. These periodic evaluations vary in how they are conducted, but most agree they are valuable in successful presidencies.

Special evaluations. Some campuses evaluate their presidents informally or sporadically. On such campuses, tensions can build and poor communication can lead either the president or the board to think that an evaluation is necessary to bring clarity to the relationship. Again, a consultant may facilitate such special evaluations because the levels of trust can be low and an objective view is helpful.

In summary, whatever process is used, honest feedback based on agreed-upon performance goals leads to successful presidencies. The process should become routine. Every evaluation influences how long and how well a presidency continues.

Chapter 36
Strategic Thinking and Planning

An important element in presidential performance is the degree to which the president's strategy for accomplishing the mission of the institution is succeeding. When a president has strong disagreements with the board or the faculty, this definitely influences the president's tenure one way or the other.

It is essential for the president and board to agree on how the key strategies aimed at accomplishing the mission are to be established. Normally, the board focuses on macro-level policies dealing with such matters as whether the budget properly funds the programs the institution plans to offer and whether the campus facilities are adequate. Its view is at 10,000 feet.

The president normally facilitates on-campus strategic planning, involving key administrators and faculty appropriately. And "appropriately" can vary widely in terms of history, campus culture, formal agreements, and personalities. When each group's role is defined and agreed upon by the other groups, strategic planning has a chance of succeeding.

Strategic planning and the results achieved are important elements of presidential and board performance reviews. When a president presses for an idea that later proves to be disastrous, his performance review naturally will suffer. It could trigger an early departure. Unfortunately, when a board presses for a particular strategy that fails, trustees generally do not resign, but a majority is usually willing to help the board make corrections in its policies dealing with strategy.

In today's fast-changing world, many argue that the ability to think strategically is more important than the ability to write a formal strategic plan every few years. Boards want a leader who can continuously assess the external and internal environments, seize opportunities, adjust to shifts in the assumptions on which a plan was based, and seek strategic alliances that help accomplish the mission. Such leadership qualities should be assessed in conjunction with how a president negotiated the last strategic plan (development of a plan usually is a requirement of accreditation).

One regular demand for strategic planning and thinking is preparation for a capital campaign, an event that is necessary every five to seven years on most campuses. Everyone has competing needs and expensive "wish lists." How the president manages this process is fair game for evaluation.

Strategic planning and strategic thinking both need to be evaluated when it is time for the president's performance review as well as when the board assesses its own performance in governance. How well this is done will affect the life cycle of presidential transitions.

Chapter 37
Getting the Right People on the Bus and in Their Places

Whether presidents leave sooner or stay longer often depends on the key people around them. Author Jim Collins's book *Good to Great* made this principle a modern management cliché: When leaders get the right people on the bus (campus) and in the right seats (assignments) success normally follows.

A president's appointment of key personnel is critical because these leaders actually have considerable authority to make a difference. This is surely true in appointing vice presidents, but often no less so in the selection of key faculty. In the long term, the quality of the faculty allows the mission to be accomplished with distinction.

While some private college boards choose to play a part in the appointment of vice presidents, this should not usually be a board role. The board might agree on which functions should be at the vice presidential level and the major responsibilities of each position, and they might set compensation limits for each slot, but the selection should be the president's task. This improves accountability, lines of authority, and loyalty. But presidents know that the board is constantly evaluating their performance on how well those invited to occupy a vice presidential seat on the bus are doing.

Most new presidents are likely to stay with existing cabinet officers for at least a year. This makes sense in many ways. The president does not know what individuals can do until they are given assignments and observed for a season. But too many presidents wait too long to ask someone to leave the bus. Most people on campus have a good sense when a vice president is not the best fit. The new president should focus on listening to others, setting short-term goals and expectations for any questionable vice president, then making the tough call sooner rather than later. Certainly, waiting three years until a poor leader finds another job or can retire is not good stewardship of this responsibility.

On some campuses, new presidents arrive and find letters of resignation from all the vice presidents. There may be planned resignations among this group, but such letters usually are deferential acts aimed at letting a new chief executive choose his own leadership team. Some president-designees signal their preference for this protocol months before taking over the helm. Ordinarily, one or two vice presidents who have known for months that a new leader will soon be on the scene will start their own search and notify the new president that they intend to leave. Whatever way it happens, new presidents often have a chance to model important leadership skills in filling vacant vice presidencies. One critical decision is whether to give an insider the chance to prove himself, even in an acting capacity for several months. The board will want to monitor this situation.

Presidents well into their service often delay too long in dismissing vice presidents they appointed. Owning up to mistakes in a timely fashion is what most boards and the campus community expect. This can be painful. Dismissing someone you selected is also a reminder to put more effort during the search to ensure that the top candidate is indeed ready for your bus and the available seat. We recommend the use of search consultants, proven assessment tools such as Myers-Briggs and Strengths Finder, and a search advisory group that can provide multiple perspectives to the president. Prior to appointment, creative ideas such as asking a top candidate to visit campus to audit a program, give a speech, critique the strategic plan, or participate in a planning meeting are worthwhile endeavors.

Faculty appointments are more difficult for presidents because their expertise is limited in most disciplines, and faculty peers want to control the selection process. In small private institutions, however, the final decision often rests with the chief academic officer. And before an offer is made, some presidents interview the finalists to ensure there is a good "mission fit." In faith-based campuses, this includes dialogue about one's faith and how that is integrated into their teaching and research. The president should not neglect this critical role in bringing the right faculty on the bus. The board's academic affairs committee also may interview finalists for full-time, tenure-track positions.

How presidents handle all personnel positions reflects their management style, their understanding of the campus culture, and how committed they are to "the bus" factor in success. Leadership styles and personal traits run the gamut from autocratic to benevolent despot to team oriented. Most presidential styles employ some of all three. Especially on small private campuses, boards should give clear signals that they want the chief executive to pay attention to who gets on the bus. A large university may be able to absorb several poor personnel decisions, but small institutions cannot.

What about administrative and staff positions that other managers hire? To be sure, the board has a role in defining, at a very macro level, some of the characteristics and expectations it has for all employees. The board should also define broad parameters for compensation, sabbatical guidelines, expectations for annual performance reviews, and so forth.

But the president can play a more active role in defining campus procedures for good search and selection practices. The president should set expectations for finding both male and female candidates who can contribute to the racial and ethnic diversity on campus, encourage training in good interview techniques, and suggest a database for future prospects.

Ultimately, who gets on the bus and in the right seat is a key responsibility of the president. And presidential performance should take this into consideration.

Chapter 38
Board Self-Evaluation and Development

A major factor in whether the top presidential candidate accepts a board's offer, how well the president interacts with the board, and whether a president is inclined to leave or stay is the degree to which the board owns its own development.

No chief executive can both report to a board and be solely responsible for its pursuit of excellence. Enlightened trustees need to help the board figure out how it develops in its own understanding and execution of its policy role and the process by which it brings new people on the board "bus." *The Nonprofit Board Answer Book* goes into many dimensions of this board responsibility; some highlights are listed here.

Every board should assign leadership for these tasks to the committee on trusteeship (other names of this committee include board development or governance committee). Here are the roles of that committee:

1. Ongoing bylaw review

2. Propose for board approval written criteria for selecting new trustees

3. Policies related to trustee selection, orientation, and evaluation

4. Nominations of board members and officers (or relations with any outside appointing authority, a function often found in religious colleges)

5. Board training

6. Evaluation of board size, structure, and process

7. Enforcement of the board's conflict-of-interest policies

The board chair is the manager of the board, the person who is accountable for the integrity of the board's process in fulfilling its governance responsibilities. How the committee on trustees evaluates this key board leader is important. Having the best chair possible not only improves the work of the board but improves the board-president relationship so critical to the success of any campus.

Every board should evaluate the president annually, but few boards take seriously the task of evaluating themselves, both as individual trustees and the board as an entity. The seriousness with which a board evaluates itself is directly correlated to the seriousness with which each trustee performs. People like to associate with successful groups, and success requires ongoing evaluation.

Here is a list of the questions a committee on trustees should consider:

1. Does the committee structure fit current needs?

2. Is each committee helping the board do its work better?

3. Are officers fulfilling their leadership roles effectively?

4. Does the board reflect the best mix of talent and experience?

5. Is a pool of prospective trustees being nurtured?

6. Has the board pursued a clear mission and major goals?

7. Has the board defined the reports it needs to measure goal achievement?

8. Are meetings informative, focused on key issues, and productive?

9. Has the board allowed the president to help it become better?

10. Does the board evaluate individual trustees based on defined expectations?

11. Have communications with faculty and staff instilled trust and confidence?

12. Is the board speaking with one voice on what it expects of the president?

13. Does the board practice the values and practices it adopted?

There are good publications from the Association of Governing Boards of Universities and Colleges (AGB), BoardSource, and others that go deeper into board evaluation and development. The purpose here is to remind boards and presidents that the "state of the board" is a critical factor in presidential transitions. The better the board, the better the chance of recruiting and keeping a good president.

Chapter 39
Major Mid-Course Adjustments

Mid-course adjustments come in two categories. First, presidents who have been in office a few years may plan an orderly review on how well things are going. Second, an important event triggers a sudden need to adjust. Examples of these events include legislative actions, accrediting agency decisions, a campus fire, or a public scandal that discredits the institution.

At the three-year mark, the president is well past the honeymoon period. A revised strategic plan is often in place, new vice presidents are in office, a capital campaign is planned or underway, enrollment trends are clear, the budget has been adjusted to reflect new realities, trustees feel they know the president—but there may be a sense that things are not going as well as everyone hoped. In today's competitive higher education market, this often occurs.

This mid-point in the normal transition cycle can be difficult. If the campus is tentative in its support of the president, a board may wonder whether it has made a mistake. But if everyone is highly satisfied with the president, the board may fear that some other campus will steal their leader. Presidents also ask themselves whether the fit is right for the long term. And they wonder how to handle feelers from search consultants.

At three or four years, it is wise for boards and presidents to agree on a thoughtful, joint mid-course review. An outside facilitator is often helpful. Maybe the president feels the need for an external evaluation (see Chapter 35). Perhaps the board feels ready to put its own responsibilities and performance under the microscope. Some would seize this period as the best time to do a better campuswide SWOT analysis (everyone looking hard at campus strengths, weaknesses, opportunities, and threats).

This is the time for boards and presidents to ask honest questions. Should the board explicitly encourage the president to think long term? Should the president tell the board that X, Y, and Z would need to happen to make a long-term commitment? This is no time for presidents to become defensive about decisions that haven't worked out. Everyone makes mistakes, and good decisions are trumped by unexpected events. This is the time to "renew the vows," so to speak, in the life-cycle of presidential leadership.

What about the unexpected events that lead to mid-course adjustments? Unfortunately, it is the rare presidency that escapes one of these events:

- A tragic fire, flood, tornado, or hurricane.

- The sudden death or resignation of the board chair, chief academic officer, or others.

- A significant drop in government or denominational financial support.

- Criminal acts or moral lapses that create public doubt.

- A freshman class that enrolls 10 percent less than the budget has projected.

For sure, some campuses celebrate over the unexpected gift of $25 million from someone not even on the A-list or a new state scholarship program that gives all needy students an extra $4,000. Maybe a faculty member's book brings national attention to your campus. Good things happen all the time, and adjusting to these good surprises is more fun. Making mid-course adjustments when the bad things happen is what can shake up a campus. This is when presidents earn their pay. The following can mitigate the downside of such events:

1. Have a good crisis-management plan, and arrange for surprise dry-runs.

2. Have a succession plan in place in the event of serious illness or death of the president.

3. Evaluate insurance policies to ensure adequate coverage for natural disasters.

4. Build an adequate unrestricted reserve fund for emergencies.

Many of the unexpected events can actually increase campus unity and commitment to rise to the occasion. Good leadership has built into the system a reservoir of goodwill that helps most people think the best of others when tough decisions are required. The board should have its own policies and procedures in place to ensure that any leadership vacuum is handled appropriately.

Chapter 40
Family, Health, and Financial Factors

Presidents have personal lives apart from their campus responsibilities. Really. Although these jobs require a 24/7 commitment, any discussion of presidential transitions needs to include critical factors that are personal to the president and his or her family. Because these by definition are unique to each situation, this list contains general examples of the types of things a president and the board should consider as part of any performance evaluation.

1. **Family.** As previously mentioned, the board should find ways to ensure housing is adequate, the needs of children are considered, and accommodations are made for any professional aspirations or responsibilities of the spouse apart from campus life. Be especially sensitive to family members with special needs, including disabilities or elderly parents who need help from a son or daughter.

2. **Health.** The board should insist on annual physical examinations for the president and perhaps membership in a health club, if campus facilities are not appropriate. Vacations and sabbaticals add value to job performance in the long run. Board chairs should assess the level of stress in the president and urge whatever adjustments make sense.

3. **Finances.** Each contract or employment agreement should reflect many of the items outlined in Chapter 19, including items that have high value to a president but may not cost much. Salary and other compensation should reflect comparisons with similar institutions so all parties feel good about what is deserved and affordable. Sometimes boards provide estate and retirement planning as a benefit.

If the board does not inquire about or anticipate the president's needs in these three areas during the annual evaluations, the president should not hesitate to bring them up. Everyone knows that these factors play a key role in assessing whether to stay or leave. A president should not let false pride keep him from candidly discussing these things. Obviously, you need to put your needs in the context of what is fair and reasonable in the eyes of campus leaders around you.

Annual evaluations and compensation reviews are the best time to raise any of these special needs. Life's circumstances change from year to year. Presidents and boards should be as creative as legally and ethically possible in addressing the personal and family needs of the president. Then the president can lead at the highest level in pursuit of the institution's mission.

In sum, evaluation of presidents and boards and campus progress and plans are all critical for institutional success. When and how these are conducted is less important than thoughtfully doing what makes sense at any point in time. Both the board and the president are responsible for taking the initiative. These are important pieces in the cycle of transitions. Do them well.

References

References Cited in this Book

Alton, Bruce T. and Kathleen Lis Dean. "Why Presidents Think the Grass is Greener," *Trusteeship*, May/June 2002, Association of Governing Boards of Universities and Colleges, Washington, D.C.

Andringa, Robert C. and Ted Engstrom. *The Nonprofit Board Answer Book*, BoardSource, Washington, D.C., 2002.

Atwell, Robert H., Madeleine F. Green, and Marlene Ross. *The Well-Informed Candidate: A Brief Guide for Candidates for College and University Presidencies*, American Council on Education, Washington, D.C., 2001.

Atwell, Robert H. and Jane Wellman. *Presidential Compensation in Higher Education: Policies and Best Practices*. Association of Governing Boards of Universities and Colleges, Washington, D.C., 2000.

Axelrod, Nancy R. *Chief Executive Succession Planning: The Board's Role in Securing Your Organization's Future*, BoardSource, Washington, D.C. 2002.

Buckingham, Marcus and Donald O. Clifton. *Now, Discover Your Strengths*, Simon & Shuster, Inc. 2001.

Collins, Jim. *Built to Last*, HarperBusiness, New York, 2001.

DiBiaggio, John A. "When to Pack It In," *Trusteeship*, November/December 1994, Association of Governing Boards of Universities and Colleges, Washington, D.C.

Edmundson, Lorna Duphiney and Gwendolyn Evans Jensen. "The Ten Guiding Principles of Presidential Transition," *The Presidency*, Winter 2003. American Council on Education, Washington, D.C.

Everley, Mary. "Supporting an Interim President," *Trusteeship*, January/February 1996, Association of Governing Boards of Universities and Colleges, Washington, D.C., 2000.

Footlick, Jerrold K. "A Steady Hand During a Presidential Crisis," *Trusteeship*, September/October 2000, Association of Governing Boards of Universities and Colleges, Washington, D.C.

Fretwell, E. K., Jr. *Advice to Interim Presidents From Those Who Have Been There*, Association of Governing Boards of Universities and Colleges, Washington, D.C., 1992.

Marchese, Theodore J. "Boards and Presidential Transitions: When a President's Departure is Mishandled, Many Campus Relationships Become Frayed," *Trusteeship*, September/October 2001, Association of Governing Boards of Universities and Colleges, Washington, D.C.

McLaughlin, Judith Block, editor. *Leadership Transitions: The New College President*, No. 93, Spring 1996, Jossey-Bass Publishers, San Francisco.

Miller, Arthur F. *The Power of Uniqueness: How to Become Who You Really Are*. Zondervan. 1999.

Moore, John W. with Joanne M. Burrows. *Presidential Succession and Transition: Beginning, Ending, and Beginning Again*. American Association of State Colleges and Universities, Washington, D.C., 2001.

Richter, Richard P. "Lame Ducks Can Leave on Wings That Fly," *Trusteeship*, July/August 1995, Association of Governing Boards of Universities and Colleges, Washington, D.C.

Viola, Joy Winkie, *Presidential Inaugurations: Planning for More than Pomp and Circumstance*. Council for Advancement and Support of Education, Washington, D.C., 1993.

Resources Recommended but
Not Specifically Referenced in this Book

Bensimon, Estela M. "Five Approaches To Think About: Lessons Learned From Experienced Presidents." In Bensimon, E.M., M. Gade & J. Kauffman, *On Assuming a College and University Presidency.* American Association of Higher Education, Washington, D.C., 1989.

Bornstein, Rita. *Legitimacy in the Academic Presidency,* American Council on Education Praeger Series on Higher Education, Westport, Conn., 2003.

Casteen, John. "Can Succession Planning Succeed?" *Trusteeship,* July/August 1995, Association of Governing Boards of Universities and Colleges, Washington, D.C.

Fisher, James L. and James V. Koch, *Presidential Leadership: Making the Difference,* American Council on Education Series on Higher Education, Oryx Press, Phoenix, Arizona, 1996. (See particularly Chapter 21 on Evaluating the President).

Gardner, David P. "Managing Transitions in a Time of Modernity," *Trusteeship,* July/August 1995, Association of Governing Boards of Universities and Colleges, Washington, D.C.

Ingram, Richard T. and William Weary. *Presidential & Board Assessment in Higher Education,* Association of Governing Boards of Universities and Colleges, Washington, D.C., 2000.

Marchese, Theodore M. assisted by Jane Fiori Lawrence, *The Search Committee Handbook: A Guide to Recruiting Administrators,* American Association for Higher Education, Washington, D.C., 1987.

Martin, James and James E. Samels, "8 Skills of Highly Effective Presidents," *Trusteeship,* September/October 2003, Association of Governing Boards of Universities and Colleges, Washington, D.C.

Martin, James and James E. Samels & Associates. *Presidential Transition in Higher Education,* The Johns Hopkins University Press, Baltimore, 2004.

McDaniel, Thomas R. "Caveats for New Presidents," *Trusteeship,* July/August 1995, Association of Governing Boards of Universities and Colleges, Washington, D.C.

Neff, Charles B. and Barbara Leondar. *Presidential Search: A Guide to the Process of Selecting and Appointing College and University Presidents,* Association of Governing Boards of Universities and Colleges, Washington, D.C., 1992.

Pierce, Susan Resneck. "Toward a Smooth Presidential Transition," *Trusteeship,* September/October 2003, Association of Governing Boards of Universities and Colleges, Washington, D.C.

There are two ways to order copies of this book.

1.   Send an email to council@cccu.org for information on ordering by credit card.

2.   Send a check made out to "CCCU" and mail it with your mailing address to:

CCCU – Presidential Transitions
321 Eighth Street, N.E.
Washington, DC 20002

Total Price Per Book

Copies	(Includes Shipping & Handling)
1	$18
2-5	$16
6-10	$14
11 or more	$12

Council for Christian Colleges & Universities
(202) 546-8713
www.cccu.org

Council of Independent Colleges
(202) 466-7230
www.cic.org